Praise for
Bring 'Em Back Alive

"Dave Burchett has tactfully tackled a tricky and serious issue in contemporary church life. Using plenty of appropriate humor and examples from Scripture to make his points, his message is both practical and powerful. If you care about the family of God, you should read this, whether you think you need to or not."

—JOHN W. STYLL, president of the Gospel Music Association

"There are few people I would trust to handle the sticky subject of bringing healing to church-wounded Christians, but Dave Burchett is most definitely one of them. With compassion, insight, firmness, and his own unique brand of humor, Dave pushes us past fruitless quibbling about who's to blame into God-honoring dialogue about what's to be done. I think I can already hear some applause from heaven"

—ANDREW MCQUITTY, senior pastor of Irving Bible Church
    in Irving, Texas

"Witty and warm, pithy and profound. If you're MIA because of church-inflicted wounds—or if you love someone who is—*Bring 'Em Back Alive* is for you. Dave Burchett has written a compelling reminder that as one of Christ's sheep, you are loved, you are wanted, and you are not alone!"

—SANDRA GLAHN, best-selling author and instructor
    at Dallas Theological Seminary

"*Bring 'Em Back Alive* challenges the reader to get involved with those who have left the church. As I read the book, I found myself arguing with Dave: 'It's to͏ ͏͏͏. T͏͏͏ ͏͏͏͏͏ ͏͏͏͏ have the time.' But with solid biblic͏ ͏͏͏͏͏ ͏ humor, and with genuine compass͏ ͏͏͏͏ convinced me that

my excuses don't matter. Christ's wandering sheep need our help. Who will reach out to them if we don't? Pastor, buy two copies of this book—one for yourself and one to give away. It's *that* good."

—DR. RAY PRITCHARD, author of *An Anchor for the Soul* and
   senior pastor of Calvary Memorial Church in Oak Park, Illinois

"I have heard it said that 'the church is the only institution that shoots its wounded.' I needed this book many times when I and my family were in the crosshairs, but there was none like it. It's my hope that when circumstances find you as the wounded, you will not run from the church, but run to its leader, Jesus Christ. He understands what being wounded is all about. In His arms you will be brought back alive!"

—RON DICIANNI, artist and author

"Dave Burchett has provided Christians with a wise and practical challenge that will bring joy and life to the church of the twenty-first century.… He gently challenges readers to become agents of God's grace so that all may experience His healing and wholeness."

—DR. STEVE MOORE, senior vice president of Asbury
   Theological Seminary

"This book is salve to wounded hearts and those with a heart for the spiritually wounded. Dave Burchett gently and compassionately provides insight and direction for the journey toward healing. His humor provides delightful moments of respite in the midst of a difficult subject. The body of Christ needs this book!"

—SUE BOHLIN, speaker, writer, and Webservant
   for Probe Ministries

"Dave Burchett…uses his own life experiences and clever wit to communicate the importance of restoring people of faith to fellowship."

—JOHN FROST, noted broadcast strategist

Bring 'Em Back
ALIVE

Bring 'Em Back
ALIVE

A Healing Plan for Those Wounded by the Church

Dave Burchett

WaterBrook
PRESS

BRING 'EM BACK ALIVE
PUBLISHED BY WATERBROOK PRESS
2375 Telstar Drive, Suite 160
Colorado Springs, Colorado 80920
A division of Random House, Inc.

ISBN 1-57856-798-X

Library of Congress Cataloging-in-Publication Data
Burchett, Dave.
     Bring 'em back alive : a healing plan for those wounded by the church / Dave Burchett.— 1st ed.
          p. cm.
     Includes bibliographical references.
     ISBN 1-57856-798-X
     1. Religious addiction. 2. Christianity—Psychology. I. Title.
     BR114.B87 2004
     253—dc22

                                                              2004004268

Printed in the United States of America
2004—First Edition

10 9 8 7 6 5 4 3 2 1

In loving memory of my father,
Paul Burchett,
who went to be with Jesus on February 6, 2004.

God's Word consistently paints an image of God as our Father. Many people struggle with that picture because they can only relate to an angry, dominating, or selfish father. I thank God I was blessed with a father who gave me a clear image of how I can relate to God as my heavenly Father.

CONTENTS

Acknowledgments xi

Introduction 1

Part I: The Heartbreak of a Scattered Flock
Naming the Pain That Drives Us Apart

1 Wounded and Abandoned 7
Caring Enough to Share Another's Pain

2 Lethargic Lambs 29
Waking Up the Flock

3 Feud for Thought 51
Uniting for the Mission

4 The Heart of a Shepherd 69
Serving Where We Are Called

5 Never Leave a Lamb Behind! 89
Mobilizing a Search-and-Rescue Team

Part II: The Wounded Lamb
A Plan for Healing and Restoration

6 Lambentations 115
Encountering Hope in Our Good Shepherd

7 Your Bleating Heart (Will Tell on You) 139
Letting Go of Victimhood

Contents

8   You Haven't Got Time for the Pain 157
Choosing to Be Healed

9   Forgiveness Is Not Optional 173
Finding Supernatural Freedom

Part III: **Reunited and It Feels So Good**
Sticking Together—Forever

10   Repeat After Me: "I Have the Right to Nothing" 193
Taking Responsibility for Ourselves and One Another

11   The Ultimate Gift of Gratitude 211
Committing to the Cause

Notes 217

ACKNOWLEDGMENTS

I gratefully acknowledge my wife, Joni, who loves me when I'm unlovable and forgives me when I'm unforgivable. You have shown me the Jesus I write about.

Thanks to my publisher and friend Don Pape for your enthusiastic support. Your belief in this project was an inspiration and encouragement. Thanks also to editorial director Laura Barker for your invaluable feedback, honesty, and sense of humor.

Special thanks to my editor Erin Healy, who inexplicably took a second project with me when it was actually your choice! Your ability to organize and clarify my ramblings is an incredible blessing. Thanks again for your humor, encouragement, and love for Jesus.

Thanks, appreciation, and love to my mom, who has always supported my crazy ideas and dreams.

Thanks and profound gratitude to my sister, Sherry, who was the first in our family to find faith in Jesus. Your step of faith has created a spiritual legacy in our family that will span generations.

Finally, thanks and love to my sons.

To Matt, thanks for your honesty and love. Your love for Jesus and others challenges and inspires me. Thanks also for bringing my beautiful daughter-in-law, Holly, into the family. I pray that the Lord will always be at the center of your marriage.

To Scott, thanks for your steadfast character and faith in the Lord. Your integrity is a remarkable testimony to your trust in Jesus. Thanks for your friendship, love, and always-honest feedback.

To Brett, thanks for your amazing heart for Jesus and others. I am touched by your caring concern for everyone around you. I look forward to watching your continuing growth into a dynamic man of God.

I am blessed by all of you.

Bring 'Em Back
ALIVE

INTRODUCTION

I don't generally receive spiritual insights during television broadcasts of women's basketball. I suspect that hardly makes me unique. But inspiration once came clearly and forcefully to me during a telecast of an NCAA women's basketball tournament game in Boulder, Colorado.

Let me set the stage for you. I am a television sports director. I call the camera shots that dictate what you see on your screen at home. Yes, I am the faceless guy whom armchair quarterbacks yell at when they want to see this shot or that reaction. On this night an undermanned (or should I say underpersoned?) Louisiana State University women's team was battling Colorado. "Battling" was the right word because LSU had only seven players dressed to play. Five key players sat injured on the bench in civilian clothes.

I selected some shots of the tired players on the court. "LSU has fought gamely with only seven players on the active roster," the announcers reported. I took a shot of the five players in street clothes. "But when these five talented contributors are nursed back to health, and you add a group of skilled recruits, LSU is going to be a powerful force next year." Then it hit me.

In the church, when injured and wounded players are sidelined, it is easy to ignore them and simply concentrate on recruiting new ones. This doesn't make a lot of sense. Let's do the math on my basketball example: Next year, if LSU returns seven players, heals the five who are injured, and brings in five recruits, they'll have seventeen able-bodied players on their roster. But if they discard the wounded, they'll have only twelve players to enter the battle.

I have watched dear friends limp away from my church "team" and have realized that my life and the body life of my church would never be quite the same. Yet no one—myself included—has gone after them. I sometimes wonder if we throw the term "church family" around a bit too loosely, because surely most of us would pursue and attempt to heal wounded members of our genetic family who wandered away.

When wounded Christians leave the church, we lose the value of their experience, skills, and wisdom. How much depth have we, the collective church, lost by not aggressively seeking to find and heal our wounded lambs?

It is not a coincidence that Scripture uses the imagery of sheep and shepherds to describe our relationships both to God and to one another. In the gospel of Matthew, we read an example from the ministry of Jesus:

> When he saw the crowds, he had compassion on
> them, because they were harassed and helpless, like
> sheep without a shepherd. (9:36, NIV)

I see God's sense of humor in His analogy. Sheep are not the brightest bulbs in the lamp store. One survey of innate animal intelligence cites sheep as being dumber than pigs, rabbits, hamsters, pigeons, and even skunks. Sheep are among the neediest of the domesticated animals, requiring constant and vigilant attention. They use their "superior" brains to repeatedly wander off the safe path into great danger, where they are essentially defenseless.

Because society has changed a bit in the past couple of millennia, we are liable to miss the nuances and power of the verses in Scripture that refer to us as God's lambs. We will explore the meaningful and important relationship between sheep and their shepherd in this book. Shepherds are totally responsible for the survival and well-being of the flock, yet the sheep seem oblivious to that constant and loving concern.

This book will examine the roles and responsibilities of the shepherds (church leaders), the flock (church congregation), and the sheep (you) when one of God's lambs is wounded. We will take an honest look at how God asks you to respond when you are the wounded lamb. And we will look at the model of the Good Shepherd (Jesus) to see how health can be restored to the wounded and how the church can be restored to wholeness.

My goal is simply to bring stray sheep back into the fellowship of other believers, an effort I will call reevangelism. Please understand that I am not talking about believers losing their salvation. I am specifically referring to the idea of returning those who have made a commitment to faith but are no longer part of a fellowship. We need to restore the wandering and injured sheep and heal them, emotionally and spiritually. And we must not ignore the uncomfortable fact that many injured lambs sit near us every Sunday. Even if they have not physically wandered off, many Christians are emotionally absent from the body of Christ, and their untended wounds are rendering them ineffective for the kingdom. They need our compassionate help too.

Imagine what could happen if we restored the powerful influence of once-committed believers and joined it with the energy of the new followers the Holy Spirit calls daily to the Lord's flock. Perhaps with that combined strength we would be more effective in our efforts to establish vibrant flocks that effectively feed and tend each sheep, as well as attract new lambs to the circle. Out in the fields, successful shepherds tend the wounded, seek the wanderers, and welcome new lambs through the miracle of birth. We Christians should do the same by pursuing the abandoned, healing and restoring our injured, and adding new lambs through the miracle of spiritual rebirth.

My prayer for how God would use this book is illustrated in a riveting scene from the movie *Black Hawk Down*. In a devastating battle, the troops have the option of escaping to safety or staying to rescue their comrades. They choose to endanger their own lives because they "never leave a man behind." Their love of country and commitment to one another prevents them from taking the easier route.

We Christians, however, are often too willing to take the easy way out and leave our brothers and sisters behind. But surely the love of God, His liberating grace, and His commitment to His bride, the church, gives us no choice but to care about and seek the lost and the wandering, the wounded, and the abandoned lambs. It is my prayer that as Christians we will come to the conviction that we must never abandon members of the flock. We are to pursue those who have been hurt or who have made bad decisions, and we have a responsibility to restore them to health, not compound their injuries. We have a call to seek those wandering lambs with the overwhelming love of Jesus. I am going to challenge you to prayerfully ask God to give you a desire to seek, comfort, and bring 'em back alive!

—Part I—

THE HEARTBREAK OF
A SCATTERED FLOCK

Naming the Pain That Drives Us Apart

Chapter 1

WOUNDED AND ABANDONED

Caring Enough to Share Another's Pain

The truth will set you free, but first it will make you miserable.

JAMES A. GARFIELD

After my first book, *When Bad Christians Happen to Good People*, was published, I braced myself for a barrage of angry criticism. I hoped those who picked up the book would honor the request of Malcolm Cowley, who asked his readers to "Be kind and considerate with your criticism.... It's just as hard to write a bad book as it is to write a good book."

In some ways it might have been easier to deal with mail from judgmental people telling me where my eternal destination is (down), how to get there (straight), and how stupid I am (very). But as He usually does, God had something different in mind for me. I still open my e-mail with fear and trembling, but for the most part my inbox has been filled with a more painful type of message. Again and again readers write to tell me their heartbreaking stories of hurt and devastation at the hands of Christians and the church.

CHASED OUT OF THE PASTURE

I try to answer every letter I get, and I hope to continue that as long as I can (or until people actually start buying my books). I try to offer a thoughtful response instead of a form letter, but tough questions with elusive answers sometimes make reaching this goal difficult. I must admit I was taken aback when I read this question:

> My husband, children and I have been brutalized
> by the church. I guess I understand why bad Chris-
> tians do bad things, but why do good Christians let
> them? I would appreciate any comments you would
> have.

What a great question! Why *do* so many of us lack the courage to get involved when our brothers and sisters suffer from the unfair, hurtful, and sinful actions of others? Anybody out there care to take that one?

Another reader poured out her anguish:

> Where is the grace? Where is the mercy? People have
> been so quick to point fingers everywhere but at them-
> selves. People have been more concerned with the
> righteousness of their cause than in giving considera-
> tion to the righteousness of their actions.

God gives this kind of wisdom to His children through suffering. What an insightful summation of the pride that wells up in so many churchgoers driving them to prove, above all else, that they are "right." This same reader made another profound observation:

> I know that mistakes have been made, but they have
> been made on both sides. (I hate that term, because if
> we are one, how can there be sides?)

Why must there be a "winner" in spiritual disputes? Isn't the very essence of our faith to love one another in a supernatural way? Part of the greatest commandment, according to our Lord, is to love our neighbors as ourselves, and He wasn't talking about just the folks who live on our block. Is there anything distinctive about a faith that prompts us to love only those who agree with us? That is not the faith that Jesus Christ came to this planet to establish. (Understand that I am not talking about disputes concerning fundamental doctrine. There are absolutes. The choice of an assistant choir director is not one of those.)

I received a copy of another letter that was slipped under my pastor's door by an angry churchgoer. He had a dispute with the pastor and shared this edifying and uplifting message:

> Shame on your family and all the people remaining
> in the church for siding with you. You and all of
> them are Hell bound!

Since I was included in the "all of them" group, I was surprised but not the least bit concerned by this stealth prophet's prediction of my own eternal destiny. He went on:

Make no mistake about it, God knows where you
are! He sees you in this time and you need fear him,
he has the power to kill you and send your soul to
Hell. Ever since the day you came, I knew you were
unholy and on your way to burn in the Lake of Fire.

I'm sure you have detected by now the theme of our little essay here. It's easy to see why so many sheep in the flock flee the pasture and keep on running. What did the author of the above missive hope to accomplish? His portrayal of God playing a cosmic whack-a-mole game with churchgoers who (in his judgment) sin is reprehensible and damaging.

Yet another letter details how a church made a painful situation worse:

My husband and I left our church after five years
of guilt-ridden manipulation. Our son, who has a
disability, was excluded and singled out within that
church. Currently we do not go to church.

This family, which needs the nurturing of a loving church, has instead been driven away.

Another former church attendee wrote:

[The situation] destroyed my faith in the church, as
well as my heart to serve. Funny thing was that the person refused to accept that he had wounded me. My side
of the story was not seen as valid at all. I left the church.
I have not found the courage to go to another yet.

This is just a small sampling of the letters I have received since the publication of *Bad Christians*. Though I am merely an author of a modestly successful book, hundreds of hurt people have contacted me to tell their stories. (You can read many of these on my Web site, www.daveburchett.com.) No doubt countless other people have either quietly wandered away from the church or chosen to live a "safe" and anonymous Christian life hidden within the flock. Both the lost sheep and those effectively crippled by other Christians are heartbreaking tragedies. Christians who do not have the freedom to be vulnerable have only limited potential to grow…or to be healed.

ONE IS THE LONELIEST NUMBER

It was never my intent to become burdened for the Lord's wounded and abandoned sheep. But I have come to care deeply about those who have been chased off as well as those who are hurt—sometimes at the hands of others, sometimes by their own doing—and are still barely hanging on.

In his wonderful book *A Shepherd Looks at Psalm 23*, Phillip Keller talks about the urgent predicament of cast sheep. *Cast* is an Old English term for a sheep that wanders off, gets itself turned over on its back, and cannot get upright. (Remember, not every little lamb can be valedictorian of the Animal Planet Network.) If not found quickly, the cast sheep might die.

Shepherds will tell you an interesting tidbit about sheep that become lost and cast. Often they are the fittest and finest of the flock. Yet they make that one mistake and find themselves and their world literally turned upside down. The parallel is striking for Christians: No matter how "mature" we believers might be, we are always in danger of flipping ourselves over. We must never think that we are above stumbling or beyond the reaches of temptation.

I shudder when I realize that King David, described in Scripture as a "man after God's own heart," committed adultery and then deceitfully and successfully plotted an innocent man's murder. Those deplorable actions resulted from one spectacular moment of weakness. Likewise, during this past year, a Christian acquaintance destroyed a thirty-five-year career and good reputation with a series of terrible and ungodly decisions. I am not above such a fate. And neither are you.

Whether chased off or cast by their own doing, many once-vibrant followers of Christ need to be loved, healed, and restored. Noted evangelical researcher George Barna made a sobering observation in his book *Grow Your Church from the Outside In* (formerly titled *Re-Churching the Unchurched*): "Relatively few unchurched people are atheists. Most of them call themselves Christian and have had a serious dose of church life in the past."[1] Apparently that "serious dose of church life"—as opposed to the healthy "body life" that Christ had in mind—has proved debilitating. In a related research report, Mr. Barna found that there are up to seventy million unchurched in our country; a staggering ten million of those are born-again Christian adults.[2] I suspect that a good percentage of those unchurched souls are wounded and abandoned lambs.

Some readers might wonder if the real problem lies with the wounded. Are they too sensitive? Aren't selfishness and pride the real reasons that people leave the church? Are they just weak? Aren't believers responsible for their own actions? Why don't these "wounded" just grow up spiritually and find a church somewhere? Some of those are fair questions, and we will discuss them throughout the book.

Those of us who have never experienced a debilitating wound, however, should be extremely careful not to judge those who have. If we have been spared pain at the hands of the flock, a fellow sheep, or a shepherd, it is by the grace of God alone. I have stumbled many times; only God has saved me from a fall. I have recovered from the wounds I have received, but I say that with no pride, only grateful realization. Those of us who are still standing shouldn't feel spiritually superior to those who are not.

SEEKING THE ONE

I love the way Jesus told stories to drive home a point. One of the parables He told was about a lost sheep and the shepherd's response to it.

As I mentioned in the introduction, I think God's sense of humor shines through His use of sheep to represent you and me. And comparing spiritual leaders to shepherds must have offended the pompous Pharisees (maybe even the sometimes-prideful disciples), because at the time shepherds were held in low esteem at Jerusalem office mixers.

The parable is found in the gospels of Matthew and Luke. A man who owns a hundred sheep discovers one is missing. Many of us think of this story as an illustration of how we are to evangelize non-Christians. I'd like you to read it with our wounded and abandoned lambs in mind.

> Look at it this way. If someone has a hundred sheep
> and one of them wanders off, doesn't he leave the
> ninety-nine and go after the one? And if he finds it,
> doesn't he make far more over it than over the ninety-
> nine who stay put? Your Father in heaven feels the

same way. He doesn't want to lose even one of these
simple believers. (Matthew 18:12-14)

Some background is valuable here. First of all, most shepherds
had small flocks, and one of their responsibilities was to count the
sheep at the end of each day. By doing so, the shepherd would immediately know if one was missing. Jesus's contemporaries would also
have known that once a sheep realized it was separated from the flock,
it would simply lie down and refuse to move (much like a teenager).
The only way for a sheep to be returned to the flock was for the shepherd to go find it and carry it back.

I find it noteworthy that lost sheep weren't expected to go looking
for the shepherd; he went looking for the sheep. The lost sheep's entire
contribution to the situation was to wander off, get lost, and then
lounge around waiting to be restored to the flock.

Sheep need constant attention. More than any other domesticated animal, sheep that are not supervised and cared for have a tendency to wander off and die. Just like our woolly counterparts,
Christians are a needy species. We tend to wander off (especially
when we're hurt), and we often don't make any effort to return.

Knowing all of this about sheep, the shepherd goes off to find
that one lost critter, leaving the ninety-nine behind. Does that mean
the ninety-nine don't matter? No; it was common practice for two to
three shepherds to tend a flock, and those listening to Jesus's parable
would have known that. But it is clear that the head shepherd, leaving the rest of the flock in the care of his helpers, takes immediate
action to find the lost sheep.

My first and admittedly hopeful response to this passage was that
the onus of finding the wandering sheep might be on the shoulders

of the head shepherd. At worst, I might have to baby-sit the flock until the shepherd returned. I was wrong. This parable is one of several in which Jesus exposed the lack of concern that the hypocritical and legalistic Pharisees displayed for the spiritually lost. And I think we, too, can extract from this parable a contemporary application for seeking the one who is wounded.

MINI-SHEPHERDS IN MEGA-FLOCKS

When a flock gets enormous, like so many churches today, the head shepherd cannot possibly count his sheep every night. The sad reality is that the contemporary church shepherd hasn't even met many of his sheep. So it becomes the responsibility of the healthy sheep in the flock to become "small-group shepherds" who regularly count their circle of sheep and—here comes the important part—who care enough to find out what has happened to those who are wandering, wounded, or cast.

I think it is interesting that the parable does not say "when" the shepherd finds the lost sheep there will be great rejoicing. This happens only "if" the sheep is found. There are no guarantees that we will find the lost sheep. So why bother? Because seeking the lost sheep is an act of obedience to God. Caring about them is an acting out of the love that He commands us to extend to one another. The prophet Ezekiel spoke about how God will seek His sheep:

> As shepherds go after their flocks when they get
> scattered, I'm going after my sheep. I'll rescue them
> from all the places they've been scattered to in the
> storms. (Ezekiel 34:12)

Clearly God cares when one of His sheep wanders away. So we must care as well. We have a responsibility as members of God's flock to seek the sheep who become separated from it.

In the parable Jesus told, it doesn't matter whether the sheep that wanders off is weak or not as valuable as the other sheep. There is no indication that the prize lamb from the Galilean County Fair generated more search-and-rescue zeal than an ugly little sheep with tattered wool. There is no suggestion that the shepherd should not or would not follow after a lamb that got lost as the result of its own foolish actions. In all likelihood (and I say this knowing how bright sheep tend to be), getting lost was a self-inflicted act of carelessness to begin with. Even so, the shepherd dropped everything to find that lost sheep.

You will notice that the shepherd didn't merely pray for God to lead the sheep back home. You will also note that the shepherd in our parable didn't ask the Lord to bring another shepherd along who would do this job for him. He also didn't speak ill of the creature and declare that the sheep could find its own way back if it cared to. Neither did the shepherd rejoice that his problem sheep had finally left, and now he could give his undivided attention to tending the good sheep. Nope. The shepherd went out and tried to find the lost sheep. And if the shepherd did find that lost one and brought it home, there was great rejoicing.

WELCOMING ARMS

Jesus's parable mentions the joy of restoring the one lost sheep that had wandered away. I realize that no joy in our faith equals that of seeing a new convert come to salvation in Christ. I would like to suggest, however, that a very close second should be welcoming a one-time devoted follower of Jesus back into the fellowship of the flock.

The story of the prodigal son is a beautiful example of how God is always waiting with open arms and ready forgiveness to restore His wandering lambs. If we desire to be like Jesus, we should follow that example and welcome them when they return.

The story is familiar: The prodigal demands his inheritance and, leaving his family, squanders it all. When he realizes his tragic mistake, he comes slinking back, expecting a severe and painful rebuke from his father. I would suspect that many wandering believers hesitate to return to the flock because they fear such a severe rebuke from other Christians—and their fears are often well founded.

The words of the prodigal son reveal his sadness as well as his fear of rejection. He knows that he has messed up royally, and he knows that whatever justice he will receive is deserved. Herein lies another key lesson for us: Most people know when they have erred. They don't need our help in realizing that fact. They do need our help to *recover* from the consequences of that bad judgment. Pastor Rick Warren once said that "most people probably know how bad they are, but they need to hear how good they can become."[3]

You can hear the desolation in the son's spirit as he speaks:

> "I'm going back to my father. I'll say to him, Father,
> I've sinned against God, I've sinned before you; I don't
> deserve to be called your son. Take me on as a hired
> hand." He got right up and went home to his father.
>
> When he was still a long way off, his father saw
> him. His heart pounding, he ran out, embraced him,
> and kissed him. The son started his speech: "Father,

I've sinned against God, I've sinned before you;
I don't deserve to be called your son ever again."
But the father wasn't listening. (Luke 15:18-22)

What an awesome description of how the father had already granted forgiveness. The son's humble return revealed the son's heart to the father, and words weren't even necessary. And this is a picture of how God has already forgiven us when we take that first step to repent and seek His forgiveness:

He was calling to the servants, "Quick. Bring a clean
set of clothes and dress him. Put the family ring on
his finger and sandals on his feet. Then get a grain-
fed heifer and roast it. We're going to feast! We're
going to have a wonderful time! My son is here—
given up for dead and now alive! Given up for lost
and now found!" And they began to have a wonderful time. (Luke 15:22-24)

So many people out there have been given up for lost. They could be found, healed, and returned. If we could only begin to communicate that we are willing to accompany them on the road back, forgive them, love them, and celebrate their return.

Scripture reveals that not everyone will be so thrilled to see the wanderers come back:

The older brother stalked off in an angry sulk and
refused to join in. His father came out and tried to
talk to him, but he wouldn't listen. The son said,

"Look how many years I've stayed here serving you,
never giving you one moment of grief, but have you
ever thrown a party for me and my friends? Then this
son of yours who has thrown away your money on
whores shows up and you go all out with a feast!"
(Luke 15:28-30)

Doesn't the older brother's response sound natural? "I have been the responsible one. I have not caused any problems. I have not wasted my inheritance, yet you throw a party for *him*."

Western ideas of fairness can too easily distort the grace, patience, and sovereign plan of God. How many times have I questioned what God is doing or thought that something He decreed isn't fair? The older son got caught—as I sometimes do—in a "rights" mentality that I will discuss in depth in chapter 10. Nevertheless, both were sons of the same father, and both received exactly what they had been promised. Still the older son thought his good behavior merited better treatment than his prodigal brother received. Surely his righteousness deserved a bit more consideration! Isn't that mind-set easy to fall into?

I hope the Holy Spirit will change our "older-brother" hearts and give us hearts to seek and find those lost, wounded, and wandering lambs. I hope He will give us an undeniable desire to bring back those who have not been so fortunate as we…and then maybe even throw a big party to celebrate their return:

His father said [to the older brother], "Son, you don't
understand. You're with me all the time, and everything that is mine is yours—but this is a wonderful

time, and we had to celebrate. This brother of yours
was dead, and he's alive! He was lost, and he's found!"
(Luke 15:31-32)

Body Politics

Most of us would gladly seek to restore *some* people to the body of
Christ. These are the people we connect with, like, and miss when
they leave. Honestly, though, we would be just as happy if others
found a different flock to call home, not because it would be better
for their growth, but because we would prefer their not being around
to bother us.

Yet Paul used the human body to illustrate how important even
the less glamorous body parts are to our own function. You might
think your big toe is not important until you break it; then you realize how vital that overlooked appendage is to everyday activities like
walking. Paul made his argument to the church at Corinth:

> Yes, the body has many parts, not just one part. If
> the foot says, "I am not a part of the body because
> I am not a hand," that does not make it any less a
> part of the body. And what would you think if you
> heard an ear say, "I am not part of the body because
> I am only an ear, and not an eye"? Would that make
> it any less a part of the body? Suppose the whole
> body were an eye—then how would you hear? Or
> if your whole body were just one big ear, how could
> you smell anything?

But that isn't the way God has made us. He has made many parts for our bodies and has put each part just where he wants it. What a strange thing a body would be if it had only one part! So he has made many parts, but still there is only one body....

Now here is what I am trying to say: All of you together are the one body of Christ and each one of you is a separate and necessary part of it. (1 Corinthians 12:14-20,27, TLB)

Clearly, every part of the body matters. Who am I to look in disdain at a member of the body that I think is not important? I find that I can easily serve and be patient with those I like. But my heart is exposed when I have to listen to someone who gives me more details than I want to hear. Or when I have to decide whether or not to minister to someone whose personality grates on me. Do I have much of an argument when I say that I don't want to restore or help heal someone because that person "annoys" me?

Scripture makes it clear that every part of the body is important. Nowhere can I find that it is my prerogative to attempt to alter the makeup of the body. Yet our treatment of wounded sheep can constitute a subtle bit of such spiritual subterfuge within the flock. (Sometimes these same actions are responsible for the wounding in the first place.) Perhaps, for example, we decide to ostracize someone who doesn't share our vision, hoping that person will take the hint and move on. Or maybe we make life a little uncomfortable for an injured lamb by creating a chilly atmosphere. And perhaps, worst of all, we make a fellow believer's life miserable by recruiting other sheep to our side of an issue.

I have to catch myself when I start thinking that I have the blueprint for how God should configure His church. Not only do I not know what each lamb can contribute to His plan, but I have no idea how God may develop a person for future service. For example, there was scant evidence in the early portions of my life that God might be preparing me to write Christian books. The truth is, the potential I see in others is often only a limited and dim vision of God's plans and hopes for them. I fear that we will be heartbroken to someday see how we Christians selfishly (or, at best, thoughtlessly) thwarted the potential that our fellow sheep possessed.

Keith Green was one of the pioneers of the contemporary Christian music movement. He once said that "it's time to quit playing church and start being the church."[4] Part of the way we can start "being the church" is by caring about *everyone* in the body, not just the humorous, the attractive, the wealthy, and the talented. God has placed every single person in each church for a reason, and it is not our job to evaluate who should be in or out of our particular flock.

It is clearly God's heart for *all* His wounded and wandering sheep to be found and returned to fellowship with the flock. Christ punctuated this truth by summing up: "In the same way your Father in heaven is not willing that any of these little ones should be lost" (Matthew 18:14, NIV).

"DOES ANYONE CARE?"

We are not dealing with new issues here, folks. Remember what Paul wrote to the Romans:

> Not everybody is ready for this, ready to see and hear
> and act. Isaiah asked what we all ask at one time or
> another: "Does anyone care, God? Is anyone listening
> and believing a word of it?" (Romans 10:16)

I would venture to guess that the very fact you are reading this book indicates you care and are willing to listen. I believe that millions of followers of Christ care about the others in the flock, but many just don't know how to show it.

"Does anyone care, God?" The plaintive cry of Isaiah hangs in the air today. Why don't we care more consistently? Sometimes we are self-centered. Perhaps we are unaware of others' needs. Sometimes we simply don't know what to do. One of the real dangers I personally face is that I sometimes adopt an attitude that says, "I'm okay; you're on your own." That works out pretty well (from my self-centered view) until I need someone who cares about me. Jesus made a simple yet earth-shakingly profound comment recorded in the book of Matthew:

> You're blessed when you care. At the moment of
> being "care-full," you find yourselves cared for. (5:7)

It is so easy for me to read the words of Jesus and then magnificently fail to understand how His wisdom applies to my daily existence. Oh, I can't give you a 100 percent guarantee that when you care, every single person will return that care. But I can guarantee that your percentages will improve dramatically, and I can throw in the added bonus of promised blessings from God. It is so incredibly simple. And since I am capable of being incredibly simple, let's review Jesus's words again:

> You're blessed when you care. At the moment of
> being "care-full," you find yourselves cared for.

My prayer is that the Lord will give every reader of this book a caring heart for the wounded and abandoned. In the chapters to come, I will lay out a plan for finding, healing, uprighting, and restoring them. The injured sheep out there present a vast, untapped resource for the church. We could contribute mightily to the cause of Christ if only we cared enough to reach out and help the injured. Some of them are cast and desperately need us to help set them upright quickly. Many are simply waiting (maybe even stubbornly) for someone to care enough to seek them out. Many are injured and still in the flock, at least for now. Some simply need to be shown the way back to the safety of the flock. Others cannot or will not be returned. But I am asking you to evaluate your heart toward wounded and abandoned lambs.

Perhaps you are a wounded lamb looking for a little hope, seeking just one good reason to return. I pray that when you close this book, you will have realized there are brothers and sisters in Christ who *do* care for you, and that you will find hope enough to return to the flock.

No "I" in Team

I live in the sports world and am fascinated by what makes a vibrant and winning team. So I'm going to share a truth from sports that offers a significant lesson to the church of Jesus Christ: A great team realizes how important every person is to the success of the organization. I can also tell you that I have rarely (and I mean rarely) seen a championship team in which every member of the team gets along perfectly with every teammate. Even the best-performing sports teams feature players who don't enjoy the company of all their teammates. Some players find a teammate or two (or more) to be irritating—or worse. Some team members never hang out together and wouldn't even consider doing so. But when that team learns how to unite for the cause of winning, something magical happens on the field or court. Petty annoyances are forgotten in their united effort to win.

Both winning and losing teams are hodgepodges of people with different backgrounds, educational levels, personality traits, and talents. But winners allow their common goal to transcend the insignificant differences, while losers allow those same traits to diminish the team's performance. One losing baseball team's lack of unity was revealed after the game when there were twenty-five players and twenty-five cabs.

Isn't it more than a little sad that we members of God's team allow meaningless differences to short-circuit the most important challenge in our lives? What could be more important than representing to the world the saving grace of Jesus Christ? When I accepted the unmerited gift of salvation by grace and began to advertise that fact, I raised the bar on how I must live my life. I won't be flawless in that effort, but choosing to live with a mediocre faith is not going to enable me to get the job done. We believers need to love, seek, return, and accept every member of our flock as we pursue the common goal of winning people to the wonderful, liberating message of Jesus Christ. It is up to the Coach to develop the plays. My job is to show up ready to be a part of the team and to contribute in whatever way He chooses to use me.

So I have a challenge for those of you who are part of the flock. I would like to enroll you in the Shepherd's search-and-rescue team.

Our aim: to restore the hurting and abandoned lambs both within and outside the church buildings. The remainder of this section will be devoted to exploring how our team can excel in that purpose.

All of us can take inspiration from Paul's words to the church at Philippi:

> If you've gotten anything at all out of following Christ,
> if his love has made any difference in your life, if being
> in a community of the Spirit means anything to you,
> if you have a heart, if you care—then do me a favor:
> Agree with each other, love each other, be deep-spirited
> friends. Don't push your way to the front; don't sweet-
> talk your way to the top. Put yourself aside, and help
> others get ahead. Don't be obsessed with getting your
> own advantage. Forget yourselves long enough to lend
> a helping hand. (Philippians 2:1-4)

God's Word is clear to me. His love has made a difference in my life. Being in the family of believers does mean something to me. And my marching orders seem pretty straightforward. He cares, and so must I. And, for the sake of the body of Christ, so must you.

— For Reflection and Discussion —

1. What responsibilities does a Christian have to seek and attempt to restore people who have been wounded by the church?
2. Read Luke 15:11-32. What applications to the process of restoring wounded lambs can you find in the story of the prodigal son?

3. In 1 Corinthians 12, Paul uses the physical body to illustrate our roles as members of Christ's body. Why do you think we tend to devalue some people and/or some roles in the church? What can we do to reverse this kind of attitude?

4. Is it a reasonable goal for every person in the church to like every other person? Is that necessary in order for a church to flourish? Explain.

5. Read Philippians 2. Write down five instructions for life in the community of Christ.

6. Think of someone you know who has left the flock. Make a commitment to pray for that person. Ask God to show you, as you proceed through this book, how you might be instrumental in bringing him or her back.

Chapter 2

LETHARGIC LAMBS

Waking Up the Flock

Thou shalt not be a victim. Thou shalt not be a perpetrator.
Above all, thou shalt not be a bystander.

INSCRIPTION AT THE HOLOCAUST MEMORIAL MUSEUM
IN WASHINGTON, D.C.

A *tlantic Monthly* columnist Jonathan Rauch recently wrote an
article declaring that America had made a major civilizational
advance. What was this remarkable achievement? That Christians
have become lukewarm and apathetic about faith in God. Rauch, an
acknowledged atheist, calls the behavior *apatheism*.

In his article, Rauch explains that apatheism is "a disinclination
to care all that much about one's own religion, and an even stronger
disinclination to care about other people's." He notes that people are
going to church less often, and when they do, they go more to social-
ize or enjoy a familiar ritual than to worship. According to Rauch, this
new breed of religious person doesn't invest much in an actual commitment to faith. The things these folks are really seeking are comfort,

spiritual reassurance, and a God who doesn't expect too much in return for their valuable time. Rauch is more than a little pleased by the trend because he believes it is better to be apathetic than to be "controlled by godly passions" for the simple reason that religion "remains the most divisive and volatile of social forces."[1] (Members of the New Testament church as described in the book of Acts would probably agree that Rauch's last statement is true.)

While I disagree with many, if not most, of Rauch's smug conclusions, I would have to agree that the behavior of many so-called Christians gives credence to his obviously biased and very disturbing accusations. Far too many Christians live lives of functional agnosticism. By that I mean that our daily behavior shows little or no evidence of a life-changing and empowering relationship with the God of the universe. Think about that for a moment: If we really believed that Jesus came to this planet to allow us to know God personally, shouldn't we demonstrate a few behavioral differences when we show up to work on Monday? Yet many of us compartmentalize our faith and fail to integrate Christ into our daily activities. Classic radio comedian Fred Allen made the wry observation that "what we really need is a faith that works the other six days of the week."

How Then Shall They Know?

One of the many ways in which I embarrass my wife is by wearing a T-shirt that says "They will know we are Christians by our T-shirts." The shirt addresses one of my pet peeves about the church. I think we like to market Jesus more than we like to make the revolutionary decision to follow Him wherever He may lead. How I wish that all of us would lose the shirts and the jewelry and concentrate on heeding the difficult and challenging words of Christ. A real commitment to following Christ would be a far more effective marketing approach than a clever bumper sticker or T-shirt.

After writing in *Bad Christians* about my disdain for the superficial marketing of Jesus, I was humbled to realize my own approach was far from flawless. I was surprised by a guest-book entry on my Web site from a longtime work associate who wrote that he "had no idea" I was a Christian. He did note that I was a good guy with a reputation for graciousness and integrity. I suppose that is better than reporting I was the south end of a northbound horse, but the statement troubled me. Shouldn't he have known without a doubt that I was a Christian?

I am going to relay an ugly truth that I trust you will keep discreetly to yourself. When I first read my colleague's comment, my pride reared up like an angry goat. Pride spoke defiantly and loudly to me: "You are a big-time Christian author now (okay, my pride is not very realistic), and you can't have people thinking that no one even recognizes you as a Christian." I was tempted to go into the Web site and delete the comment so that no one would have any doubts about my faith.

But I came to the conclusion that the problem did not originate with my friend; the problem was with me. I chose to leave the comment, and I considered instead what I could do to represent Christ in such a way that my love for Him would not go unnoticed. I was saddened that someone could know me for as long as my associate had and not be aware that Jesus is the center of my universe.

I don't propose that we stand on street corners with bullhorns and sandwich boards to let the world know we believe in Jesus. Instead common sense and some very discomforting scriptures lead me to believe that a life-changing relationship with Jesus should show. For the record, may I offer the following exhibits?

> If you love me, show it by doing what I've told you. (John 14:15)

> Show them what you're made of, the love I've been talking up in the churches. Let them see it for themselves! (2 Corinthians 8:24)

> I keep hearing of the love and faith you have for the Master Jesus, which brims over to other Christians. (Philemon 1:5)

Whatever is at the core of our hearts—whether Christ or golf or gardening—will be evident to those who spend even a modest amount of time with us. My desire is to make sure that those around me know that my faith in Christ is paramount to who I am. Achieving this goal—and avoiding Jonathan Rauch's apatheism—has been a point of emphasis in my recent faith journey.

SHEEP WHO SLEEP

So what was the reason for my friend's surprise? I believe that for too many years I was a lethargic lamb. Oh sure, I was a member in good standing within the flock, but I no longer displayed the exuberance that came so naturally after I first experienced forgiveness and salvation in Jesus.

How does lethargy set in? I wish I cared enough to tell you. (Rim shot, please.)

Seriously now: I would venture that none of us enters into Christianity planning to fail. We desire the forgiveness, the peace, and the love of Christ, and we want all this to be evident in our daily lives. Most of us start out with genuine excitement and real joy about our faith. Yet I have had the sad experience of observing the giddiness of new believers in Jesus and noting to myself that they will come back to earth soon. But why should they?

Why did I?

There was a time when I wanted to hold on forever to that feeling of acceptance, peace, and forgiveness. I desired to love others as Jesus loved me. What happened? Well, the remarkable relationship between sheep and shepherd will again prove instructive to our spiritual walk. To follow are nine reasons why lambs become lethargic.

1. Their Pastures Are Barren

Sheep left unsupervised will overgraze a field until it is barren. Instead of moving on, the sheep will devour the vegetation and literally destroy any chance that the field will regenerate. The shepherd knows he must keep his flock moving to a new place, a different pasture, in order to ensure nourishment and health.

Application: Like sheep, we are creatures of habit. We tend to get into ruts that can be deadly to our spiritual growth. I must hasten to note that avoiding a rut doesn't mean bouncing from church to church or always looking to find a more entertaining shepherd. The rut I'm talking about is that comfortable spiritual plateau on which we like to stay put. We graze at the same (or at a lower) level of knowledge and commitment. We are reluctant to participate in challenging Bible studies or accountability groups, or to give sacrificially of our time or resources. We may be unwilling to take chances or be stretched. The next thing we know, there is nothing left in the field to provide us with new spiritual nourishment. Even so, we will stubbornly continue to graze in that safe place.

Staying at one comfortable level is not possible for those who are in a dynamic relationship with God. Based on my own experience, I can confidently say we are either moving forward or falling behind in our walk with Christ. Certainly taking a step backward now and then is part of the process of maturity. But there can be no status quo in a faith-walk with Jesus: We are moving either forward or backward. The simple truth is, it's hard to keep growing in a barren pasture.

2. They're Drinking from Polluted Wells

Most animals will only drink polluted water out of dire, life-saving necessity. But sheep will drink anything when they're thirsty. They will drink from parasite-infested water without reservation if they are not led to clean, safe water.

Application: We are spiritual beings, created by God to be spiritually thirsty. Our desire to quench that thirst can lead us in some amazing, misguided directions that we will discuss later. Sheep that are thirsty will become restless and, if no shepherd is watching over them, will wander off in search of water. Any water. The sheep without a shepherd will go after the most immediate source with absolutely no concern for disease or the discomfort that tomorrow might bring. Sheep want their thirst satisfied immediately, and it is the shepherd's job to make sure the thirst is quenched safely.

For various reasons, many of us in today's churches are spiritually thirsty. Some of us suffer from poor teaching. Others never received proper discipleship in the fundamentals of the faith. Some lack knowledge about how to study God's Word and apply that knowledge to their daily lives. Others are simply lazy or uninterested in making the required commitment. Perhaps some are engaged in a sin that is a little too appealing to give up. And some confuse the normal ups and downs of the spiritual journey with total failure and give up.

One professional athlete told me that he was unwilling to give up the women who make themselves readily available to sports stars. He knew in his heart that his behavior was wrong, but he was simply not willing to allow Christ to illuminate that area of his life because he feared that he would have to give it up. The irony, of course, is that faith in Jesus does not take anything away from our lives without replacing it with something better. The athlete was not able to see that his thirst for intimacy was only temporarily numbed by the one-night stands. That's why he didn't feel right about his behavior even as he refused to give it up.

In an odd way this man's restless search for intimacy can be considered a genuine search for intimacy with God. It was G. K. Chesterton who noted, "the man knocking on the brothel door is really searching for God." That seems like quite a strange statement until you consider how we were created. Recent scientific research suggests that our brains are hard-wired to seek spiritual things. Some professionals believe this is some sort of evolutionary self-delusion, a need to take false comfort in an invented higher power. My take is a little different: I know that I am wired to desire a relationship with my Creator. Whether that truth is hard-wired in my brain or written across my heart doesn't matter, but my thirst can be satisfied only by pure, Living Water.

3. They're Restless and Unsupervised

A restless and unsupervised sheep will lead itself and others into danger. Those who raise sheep will tell you there is always that one sheep that simply will not stay put. And when it wanders, that sheep takes others with it.

Application: Like a thirsty sheep, a bored and unfulfilled Christian who is without spiritual shepherding may wander onto paths that lead away from God. And that unfulfilled and restless lamb may convince others to follow. Shepherding is a part of God's plan for us, and ideally it should occur within the fellowship of a flock. I came upon the following wonderful description of the need for shepherds. Author Lena Wolter wrote, "A shepherd is needed only when there are no fences. He is someone who stays with his sheep at all costs, guiding, protecting and walking with them through the fields. He's not just a person who raises sheep."[2] She went on to describe leaders who build fences around their flock as "mutton farmers." Ms. Wolter theorized that some leaders build fences around their sheep so they won't have to get their feet dirty chasing their sheep through open fields. My experience with legalistic and controlling churches certainly validates that theory. Those leaders burden the sheep by demanding that they follow every rule precisely, or else they will surely suffer because of their failing. You can build the electric fence of legalism around the flock to control it, but that shepherding approach will rarely lead to healthy sheep.

We human beings are prone to wander, just like that bored and restless lamb, whenever we try to get by on our own. Knowing that we need shepherds who do not fence us in and who are willing to get their feet dirty, Jesus ordained the church to be our shepherding structure. We shortchange our walk if we ignore or deny that fact. I

acknowledge that many churches have failed in this responsibility, but that doesn't change the truth that thousands of others are lovingly shepherding their flocks. Also, I believe that God honors the prayerful persistence of sheep who are looking for a healthy flock.

4. They Are Type A, Self-Centered Animals

Sheep are almost incapable of relaxing. They are timid and constantly fearful of predators. They are easily distressed by friction within the flock. (Does the Lord know us or what?) They get irritable and grumpy when flies and parasites bother them.

Application: In order to be temporarily happy, a lamb has to feel secure, sense no division in the flock, suffer no pests, and have a full belly. Does that sound like the First Church of Everywhere to you? Naturally, too much emphasis on personal comfort within the flock can lead to self-absorption. And it doesn't take a genius to deduce that self-absorption is a symptom of pride. Pride takes our eyes off of Jesus, and anytime that happens, we are at risk of slipping into spiritual lethargy.

5. They Deny Their Need for Leadership

Sheep depend on the shepherd in order to thrive, but they are too dumb to know it.

Application: I don't even have to say it, do I? Seriously, a big part of our lethargy comes from not understanding our relationship to the Good Shepherd. I will explore this truth in greater detail in chapter 6.

6. They Are Spiritually Out of Shape

Though fit sheep can sometimes be cast, fat sheep, frankly, are *likely* to be cast. If not for the tragic possibilities, it would be a humorous

sight to see a fat little sheep upside down with its legs helplessly flailing. As I mentioned in chapter 1, the unfortunate victim will suffer circulation loss, dehydration, and possibly death if not found quickly.

Application: I suppose being fat and easily cast (turned from the faith) has been a factor throughout the ages, but it's hard to imagine that it was ever more of an issue than in present-day America. We have become spiritually (and, yes, physically) fat, easily overturned because faith in this country is just too easy. Acknowledging Christ in America is essentially risk free. A bit of ridicule is the most that the average Christian might have to endure, and that is nothing when compared to what Christians endure in nations where violent persecution of Christianity is the norm. When you have to decide if Jesus is worth jail, abuse, or worse, you are not so likely to be fat, sassy, and easily cast. I am sensing a much-needed stirring from our lethargy over many vital cultural issues. In late 2003 the Christian community has rightly been heard on debates over partial-birth abortion and the heartbreaking fight over removing the feeding tube from incapacitated but not comatose patient Terri Schiavo. I am inspired by the Christians who "get it," who understand that we are in a cultural spiritual battle that requires us to abandon lethargy and live for Christ.

7. They Need Time to Heal but Often Can't Get It

When a cast or overturned sheep is found, the shepherd cannot simply flip 'em over and move on. A once-cast sheep must be handled carefully until proper circulation is restored and it can return to its former level of activity. That might explain the wonderful picture of the shepherd returning with the lost sheep on his shoulders until the frantic animal can walk on its own.

Application: Christians sometimes become lethargic because they feel they cannot be restored and/or healed from hurts, and this sends them into a spiritual depression of sorts. Christian friends are often a lot like Job's running buddies who offered simple and quick fixes (not to mention wrong ones) instead of a compassionate ear, a loving heart, and a caring touch. When I find my friends in trouble, I am usually agreeable to flipping 'em over, but please don't ask me to carry them on my shoulders. I have my own problems, you know, and it's a burden to carry a wounded sheep. It's an imposition to lovingly restore an injured lamb to the body. Nevertheless, we "friends" need to learn how to do that. More important, we need to ask God to give us the *desire* to do that.

8. *They Isolate Themselves Unnecessarily*

Sheep are made to be together. The sheepherder's code of recommendations for the welfare of sheep advises that the sheep not be isolated from other sheep for longer than absolutely necessary.

Application: We are kidding ourselves when we think we can fully grow in Jesus as a Lone Ranger Christian. Of course if we are forced to be alone, God will meet us in that circumstance, but we are not to choose isolation as the ideal growth medium for spiritual maturity. We were created to follow the Shepherd within a flock with other Christians. At times it might seem easier just to go it alone. I have talked to many believers who feel it would be simpler to be a Christian outside of the church. In fact, some teachers are proclaiming that the church age is over. But John Wesley said, "No one can be a Christian alone." And I don't believe he was talking about basic salvation; I believe he was talking about experiencing the fullness and vitality that Jesus intended us to know when we are immersed in the richness of His community. It is the system He set up and ordained. We should not choose to remove ourselves from the flock, though I understand the desire to do exactly that.

Some wounded people take such a "never again" approach to love relationships or friendships. I can promise those who have that attitude that they will never be hurt. They can choose to never trust and confide in a friend, and they will have no friend to disappoint them. A dear friend of mine (who had been wounded by a friend) wrote to me and asked if I could still trust my heart to anyone outside of immediate family. I told him that I counted only a handful of people whom I could truly trust with my heart. But having just one person who accepts me exactly as I am is a small earthly taste of God's grace.

If you choose not to risk trusting another person, you will never experience the fullness of love and all that life has to offer. The same risk applies when you remove yourself from the flock and refuse to ever trust another Christian. Yes, being vulnerable in the church is a risk. Yes, churchgoers may fail you and will likely cause you some pain along the way. But when you find a fellowship of believers that loves and accepts you, you will take a healing dip in the pool of grace and experience a little preview of heaven.

9. They Burn Out Easily

The same sheepherder's guidelines note that sheep must not be forced to proceed at a pace likely to cause stress or exhaustion.

Application: I think there are a couple of applications here. The first points to the danger in our tendency to burn out a new and zealous believer. It is easy to get caught up in the enthusiasm and joy of new Christians and get them involved in everything. Plus, they are so willing to do anything. But mature members of the flock must realize that new believers need time to learn and grow. Most churches could benefit by prayerful and careful measures to prevent new believers from becoming involved in too much too soon. We should be mindful that any Christian is a target for overcommitment and burnout. Remind others—and yourself—to maintain a balance that allows for personal, family, and community time.

The other application is a bit more subtle. (And I am, as you have realized, Mr. Subtle.) I run into Christians who try to make others in the fellowship be just like them, a pressure that can put a lot of stress on a young believer. The goal of discipleship is not to make one believer act and think just like another. Yet some of us try to force our fellow believers to accept our personal agendas and convictions as doctrine. Allowing a young believer to take on too much, or forcing one to adopt another's personal convictions, can lead to lethargic lambs.

How Lethargy Leads to Injury

"I guess I understand why bad Christians do bad things, but why do good Christians let them?" Now that you've had some time to think on that challenging question, I'm going to take a stab at an answer: Lethargic lambs are more likely than lively lambs to stand by idly while other lambs are attacked or wounded. This is in part a culturally related phenomenon. We have been conditioned not to get involved. When your mama taught you that other people's troubles are "none of your business," I don't think she meant you should be a spectator when others are maligned or attacked, especially in the church. As messy as it can be, we need to correct sheep that bite. We are responsible for defending our fellow Christians against attack. But when we are lethargic, this task of helping our brothers and sisters seems difficult and sometimes even impossible.

Scripture offers clear warnings against abusing our fellow sheep. First, the words of Jesus in Matthew:

> I'm telling you that anyone who is so much as angry
> with a brother or sister is guilty of murder. Carelessly
> call a brother "idiot!" and you just might find your-
> self hauled into court. Thoughtlessly yell "stupid!"
> at a sister and you are on the brink of hellfire. The
> simple moral fact is that words kill. (5:22)

I am going to tell you a story about a little boy with a terrible temper. His father gave him a big bag of nails and instructed him to hammer a nail into the fence every time he lost his temper. On the first day the little boy hammered more than three dozen nails into the fence. But as the days went by, the boy began to control his temper more and more. One day the young man realized that he was no longer driving nails into the fence. When he proudly told his father, he was given the new task of pulling out one nail for every day he continued to hold his temper. Finally all of the nails were removed. Then the father took his son out to the fence. "You have done a great job, son. But look at the holes in the fence. This fence will never be like it was before. When you say things in anger, they leave a scar just like this one. You can stick a knife in a person, and no matter how many times you say I'm sorry, the scar will stay there. A verbal wound is just as bad as a physical one."

We don't think about that much, do we? I know that I have

sometimes inflicted wounds with words and didn't even know it. Forgive me for my lack of awareness. As you might have already guessed, this is an ongoing battle in my corner.

Next, the apostle Paul weighs in with some typically strong admonitions:

> So where does that leave you when you criticize a
> brother? And where does that leave you when you
> condescend to a sister? I'd say it leaves you looking
> pretty silly—or worse. Eventually, we're all going to
> end up kneeling side by side in the place of judg-
> ment, facing God. Your critical and condescending
> ways aren't going to improve your position there one
> bit. (Romans 14:10)

Is there anyone else squirming besides me? At the risk of sounding like another bad infomercial: Wait, there's more! This time from the apostle John:

> Here's how you tell the difference between God's chil-
> dren and the Devil's children: The one who won't
> practice righteous ways isn't from God, nor is the
> one who won't love brother or sister. A simple test.
> (1 John 3:10)

It is a simple test, isn't it? Can we really claim that Jesus is changing our very hearts yet still harbor ill feelings against people in the church? As if John hadn't made me uncomfortable enough, later in the same chapter he writes:

> If you see some brother or sister in need and have
> the means to do something about it but turn a cold
> shoulder and do nothing, what happens to God's
> love? It disappears. And you made it disappear.
> (1 John 3:17)

Forgive the long pause. I was taking a standing eight count and sniffing smelling salts after that last scriptural punch.

I realize that some people want to get involved in everyone's business. I am not talking about becoming people who always insert themselves where they are not welcome. I am talking about being a Christian who cares enough to be willing to, at the very least, be inconvenienced for the sake of a fellow child of God. I think that we followers of Christ have an obligation to extend ourselves to our hurting brothers and sisters in the faith with prayer and other practical support.

Elie Wiesel wrote powerfully about the tragedy of the Holocaust. Among his astute insights is this observation: "The opposite of love is not hate. The opposite of love is indifference."[3] His words rocked me back on my heels. I found myself convicted and humbled, for though I had prided myself on *not hating,* I had effectively done as much damage by *not acting.* And that is the real tragedy of apatheism and lethargy—indifference toward struggling, wounded, and abandoned lambs.

WOLVES IN SHEEP'S CLOTHING

I have saved one more reason we often become lethargic lambs: For many of us, the behavior of our fellow flock members frustrates us to the point that we resign ourselves to simply going through the motions of worship, fellowship, and other spiritual disciplines.

The acts of many who claim to be Christians are simply indefensible. Perhaps we need to consider calling these folks "people in the church" rather than "Christians." I often hear laments from wounded lambs who ask, in effect, "How could a Christian do something like this?" It seems pretty clear that a follower of Christ who is abiding in Him wouldn't do something like that. (In some cases, Christians who wound are crawling through a spiritual desert of their own. They might do or say something during an arid time that they would be horrified to recall in better spiritual times. Grace and forgiveness go a long way for everyone in such instances.) In truth, "people in the church" who attempt to live in their own strength apart from Christ are apt to behave exactly like anyone outside the faith.

Jesus clearly warned that there would be many among us who, to be candid, are not really on the team. That is why I would prefer that we use "people in the church" when we describe those who wound others. I fear that those who always label their attackers as "Christians" may find it increasingly difficult to distinguish between those who are genuinely trying to follow Jesus and those who really do not understand or even know Him.

Researcher George Barna found that over 43 percent of the adults who attend Christian church services in a typical week are not born-again Christians.[4] Without throwing down a percentage, Jesus presented a parable that said pretty much the same thing:

> The kingdom of heaven may be compared to a man
> who sowed good seed in his field. But while his men
> were sleeping, his enemy came and sowed tares among
> the wheat, and went away. But when the wheat sprouted
> and bore grain, then the tares became evident also.
>
> The slaves of the landowner came and said to
> him, "Sir, did you not sow good seed in your field?
> How then does it have tares?"
>
> And he said to them, "An enemy has done this!"
>
> The slaves said to him, "Do you want us, then,
> to go and gather them up?"
>
> But he said, "No; for while you are gathering
> up the tares, you may uproot the wheat with them.
> Allow both to grow together until the harvest; and
> in the time of the harvest I will say to the reapers,
> 'First gather up the tares and bind them in bundles to
> burn them up; but gather the wheat into my barn.'"
> (Matthew 13:24-30, NASB)

When we Christians in our culture read this story, we might react like Noah in comedian Bill Cosby's famous routine about Noah and

God. God instructs Noah concerning the boat's exact dimensions, saying, "The length of the ark shall be three hundred cubits, the breadth of it fifty cubits, and the height of it thirty cubits" (Genesis 6:15, KJV). Cosby imagines Noah's replying, "Right. [Long pause.] What's a cubit?"

When I read the passage about the tares, my first response was something along the lines of, "Right," followed by a Cosby-like pause, then, "What's a tare?" Well, dear reader, a little Internet time revealed that a tare is any of various weedy plants of the genus *Vicia*, especially the common vetch. (You will be tested on this material.) In Syria and Palestine where Jesus taught, the tare, known as the bearded darnel, grows plentifully. Of particular interest is how the plant develops: It bears an uncanny resemblance to wheat until the head appears on the plant. Only then is the difference easily discerned.

What an incredible word picture that story painted for people in an agrarian society. The weed appeared to be wheat—even an experienced farmer could not tell the difference—until the time came for it to produce fruit. Only then was its true nature revealed. To have attempted to weed it out sooner would have been impossible, and attempting to do so would have destroyed valuable grains. Only time would tell if the plant was the real deal or the nuisance imposter. And so to my point: Much damage to the church and to other believers is done by the "tares" that are sown in the fields of Christianity.

Do you have any guesses concerning the identity of the enemy who sows the congregational tares? If I may borrow from the Dana Carvey Church Lady character: "Could it be [echo] *Satan?*" How the satanic realm must rejoice when the actions of a tare cause someone to leave faith behind. Is it so hard to imagine that the spiritual battle raging around us would involve spiritual double agents in the church? That seems like a good war plan to me. The Enemy understands our nature and how to infiltrate our fellowships.

AN IMPORTANT WORD OF CAUTION: I am not suggesting that we set up tare-hunting committees to identify who is "in the kingdom" and who is out. And I am certainly not suggesting that any person in the church who makes a mistake or hurts someone is not a Christian. That is not for us to judge. Instead, I am suggesting that we consider the possibility that some wounds are perpetrated by non-Christians or by "believers" who are not truly walking in Christ.

LEAPING LAMBS

We were not created to be lethargic lambs. University of Pennsylvania psychologist Martin Seligman said: "Human beings want to have meaning. They do not want to wake up in the morning with a gnawing realization that they are fidgeting until they die." Each of us has a hard-wired, deep-seated yearning for intimacy with God. That is why being a lethargic lamb is so depressing. We know instinctively that much more is available to us.

So if you are tired of moping around the pasture like a lethargic lamb, decide to change. The power is available. That's right, ladies and gentlemen: an amazing biblical elixir guaranteed to lift you from lethargy and make you a lively lamb again! Seriously, you don't have to remain a lethargic lamb, painfully shuffling through the motions of faith. The Good Shepherd has a cure for us, and it starts with His prescription for unity.

— For Reflection and Discussion —

1. Do you agree with writer Jonathan Rauch, who believes that Christians have become apathetic? Why or why not? What are some signs of apathy that we Christians should be on guard against?

2. Is it reasonable to expect that anyone who knows you should know you are a Christian? Why or why not? What can you do to make your faith known without driving people away?

3. Read the three verses on page 32. Name several practical ways in which you could "show others what you're made of."

4. From the list on pages 33-41, what is the number one factor that might cause you to be a lethargic lamb? What will you do to avoid this particular pitfall?

5. Read Matthew 5:22. Why do we so often fail to understand the damage caused by our careless words?

6. Review the three verses on pages 43-4. What can we do to develop a more humble and loving attitude toward one another in the church?

Chapter 3

FEUD FOR THOUGHT

Uniting for the Mission

It isn't that they can't see the solution. It is that they can't see the problem.

G. K. CHESTERTON

The best way to model Christ is both ridiculously simple and maddeningly difficult. In John 15, Jesus proclaims, "My command is this: Love each other as I have loved you" (verse 12, NIV). The apostles' reaction must have been about like mine: "Yeah, sure, whatever, Lord…but you haven't met Bob." Five verses later Jesus repeats the simple command for us slow and/or stubborn children: "Love each other." How we have complicated that wonderful and basic instruction.

Shepherds will tell you that sheep are just as prone to jealousy and strife as their human counterparts. Culturally, we speak of the pecking order of a social club or business. When speaking of a flock, we can instead speak of the "butting order." Phillip Keller's wonderful description of this concept has an almost comical parallel in the church: "Generally an arrogant, cunning and dominating old ewe will be the boss of any bunch of sheep. [Too easy... Show restraint, Dave!] She maintains her position of prestige by butting and driving the other ewes or lambs away from the best grazing or favorite bedgrounds." (I would never stoop to compare this behavior with demanding to sing the cantata solo or lead the women's ministry.) According to Mr. Keller, the ewe's rivalry and competition for status damages the health of the flock. "The sheep become edgy, tense, discontented and restless." His next observation paints a beautiful picture of how Jesus should function as the Good Shepherd within our own church flock. Mr. Keller marveled that whenever he (the shepherd) came into view, the sheep would abandon their foolish rivalries and quit fighting.[1] If only we had the faith to invite Christ into our foolish rivalries, we would no doubt stop butting and start loving.

I remember a public-service announcement from my youth that addressed speeding on the highways. In the television commercial, the old family station wagon (for you young uns, that was a prehistoric SUV) was toolin' down the road above the posted speed limit. Suddenly the driver would see the ghostly image of a police car. This phantom police car would prompt the driver to slow down and think about the safety of his family and the importance of obeying the laws. The tag line was "Remember the phantom police car." That image has remained with me all these years. If we could only see the living Christ (not a phantom) in situations where our pride wants to take over, perhaps we would also see the importance of remembering His commands and following Him. Living with a keen awareness of His presence seems to be an ongoing spiritual challenge for me, and probably for you as well. That awareness would certainly help us in our struggles to love our neighbors.

The Feud Pyramid

In the book of Jude, we read words that could have been written in last month's *Christianity Today:*

> "In the last days there will be people who don't take
> these things seriously anymore. They'll treat them like
> a joke, and make a religion of their own whims and
> lusts." These are the ones who split churches, think-
> ing only of themselves. There's nothing to them, no
> sign of the Spirit! (Jude 18-19)

We believers love to talk about multiplication (church growth), but we really only seem to understand division. The Bible accepts no excuses for being part of any division within the church. Paul makes a succinct point (he tended to do that) about division in the church at Crete:

> But avoid foolish controversies and genealogies and
> arguments and quarrels about the law, because these
> are unprofitable and useless. Warn a divisive person
> once, and then warn him a second time. After that,
> have nothing to do with him. You may be sure that
> such a man is warped and sinful; he is self-condemned.
> (Titus 3:9-11, NIV)

That warning about self-condemnation humbles and quite frankly frightens me. Paul does not mince words. To paraphrase a popular T-shirt slogan: "What Part of NO [Division] Do You Not Understand?"

About ten years before his letter to Titus, the apostle wrote a difficult letter of rebuke to the church of Corinth. The Corinthian church, as we say, "had issues." Among the problems: gross sexual misconduct, intellectual arrogance, division among the body, and false teachings on basic doctrines. I would suspect a typical congregation's ranking of the importance of these same offenses today might look something like this:

Behavior Requiring Correction and Total Condemnation

Sexual Misconduct	75%
False Teachings	20%
Intellectual Arrogance	3%
Division	2%

Can't you just imagine the board meeting in Corinth before Paul's letter arrived? Just like in the movies, these Corinthians conveniently speak contemporary English:

Corinthian 1: "I am worried about the unity of our body."

Corinthian 2: "How can you possibly be worried about that with all this sexual sin going on? You are just as big a sinner as they are if you don't agree with me!"

Corinthian 3: "Well, *I* agree. We have an obligation to split the church in order to purify it and get rid of these wicked sinners!"

Corinthian 1: "But can't we be united in the love of—"

Corinthians 2 and 3: "NO!"

The manner in which Paul addressed these same issues is instructive. Remember, he fearlessly confronted any issue, anytime, anywhere. Yet his first appeal was not to stop the sexual immorality or false teaching. He first addressed division:

> I appeal to you, brothers, in the name of our Lord
> Jesus Christ, that all of you agree with one another
> so that there may be no divisions among you and
> that you may be perfectly united in mind and
> thought. My brothers, some from Chloe's household
> have informed me that there are quarrels among you.
> What I mean is this: One of you says, "I follow
> Paul"; another, "I follow Apollos"; another, "I follow
> Cephas"; still another, "I follow Christ." Is Christ
> divided? (1 Corinthians 1:10-13, NIV)

I like the way the last phrase is rendered in the *New Living Translation,* which asks, "Can Christ be divided into pieces?" That is literally what we do when we divide a church. Pride and the desire to be right tear apart the unity that our Lord commanded. His Word is clear. Division within the body of Christ is sin. Jesus's teaching about unity is indisputable.

JESUS'S FINAL PRAYER FOR US

The night before He was betrayed and turned over to His accusers, Jesus prayed. His prayer is recorded in John 17. First the Lord prayed for Himself, then for His disciples, and then for all believers. Below is a portion of Jesus's final prayer for you and me. It was spoken just hours before He was arrested, in short order to be tried and crucified. Take a moment to consider the context of this prayer. When you know your time is short, you will say only what is most important and let the superfluous fade away. Christ knew exactly what was coming, and it stands to reason that this final prayer reflects what weighed most heavily on His heart. It was a prayer for unity:

> I pray also for those who will believe in me through
> [the disciples'] message, that all of them may be one,
> Father, just as you are in me and I am in you. May
> they also be in us so that the world may believe that
> you have sent me. I have given them the glory that
> you gave me, that they may be one as we are one:
> I in them and you in me. May they be brought to
> complete unity to let the world know that you sent
> me and have loved them even as you have loved me.
> (John 17:20-23, NIV)

I am not a big proponent of shoveling guilt on the brethren. There are others far more skilled at that task (and I have met many of them). But I must say that we have really dropped the ball on this one. I am sobered when I reflect on the agony that Christ endured shortly after praying for us to be unified in Him. I realize the critical importance that He placed on Christians modeling unity and thereby reflecting His presence to an unbelieving world. In my half-full optimism, I must admit we can't be flawless. But even if I were a half-empty pessimist, I am quite sure that we can do better.

It has become increasingly apparent to me why Jesus placed unity at the top of His prayer list for the church. Our heartrending lack of unity is a deterrent to faith for those inside as well as outside the church. I received the following letter lamenting how faith is perceived by family members outside the church:

> My husband is the only Christian in his family—we've been told on several occasions that we're crazy to pursue our "religion" when this is the kind of thing (wounding each other) our "brothers and sisters" do to one another. They want absolutely nothing to do with the body of Christ. Quite frankly, sometimes neither do we.

We have allowed Satan to gain the beachhead in the spiritual war for church unity. I suspect that the war-room strategists from Hades agree with the statement of General Napoléon Bonaparte: "Never interrupt your enemy when he is making a mistake." I am pretty sure the demonic leadership is well pleased with their progress on this battlefield.

UNITED WE STAND, DIVIDED WE FAIL

Before we can effectively address the issues of woundedness, forgiveness, and healing, we must be committed to seeking unity in the body of Christ. Division in the church hampers our ability on many levels to seek wounded lambs. Most notably, however, fighting among the flock diverts the ostensibly healthy sheep from almost everything else except the ongoing feud. When such counterproductive behavior persists, can those of us in the fray really focus on loving and pursuing the wounded lambs? I know from sad personal experience how spiritually and emotionally debilitating church division can become.

A wounded lamb that observes the sheep nipping at each others' behinds is unlikely to return. And if that injured sheep does tentatively stumble back, why would it want to stay?

Pardon me while I rant. Can we not see that we are playing right into the Enemy's hands when we allow generally honest and sincere disagreements to escalate into a civil war? Missionary E. Stanley Jones noted, "When we talk about what we believe in, we divide. When we talk about Who we believe in, we unite." Is it too much for Christians to concentrate on the One we believe in long enough to make a difference in this world? I'm sorry, but today's church seems as bent on persnickety bickering and division as our political leaders do. We tend to blame everybody else for our society's moral decline, when actually *we* hold the key in our collective hands to rev up a culture-changing revival. The petty partisanship of the church boils my blood, and I hope you will join up in not taking it any more. (End of this particular rant; resume normal reading.)

Frederick Buechner, in his book *Whistling in the Dark,* writes about the possibility of living in harmony despite our differences. "There's no reason why everyone should be Christian in the same way and every reason to leave room for differences, but if all the competing factions of Christendom were to give as much of themselves to the high calling and holy hope that unites them as they do now to the relative inconsequentialities that divide them, the Church would look more like the Kingdom of God for a change and less like an ungodly mess."[2] He's a more articulate ranter than I, but we share the same opinion: We need to cede control to the Savior and let Him sort out the rest.

No More Family Feud Reruns

I am not naive enough to think that we can solve everything with a New Year's resolution. We are flawed and we are sinners, and we bring to the party everything those two truths imply. But I do believe in the power of the Holy Spirit and the always-present possibility of revival in the body of Christ. So I will remain a prayerful optimist until the Lord takes me home.

To follow is my modest step-by-step plan to begin to shift the momentum in our battle for unity.

1. Remember That Christ Died for Everyone

The reality of this truth can make a person uncomfortable. That guy who hits his wife: Christ died for him. The homeless guy in the refrigerator box under the bridge, the rebellious kid with the pierced nose and eyebrow: He died for them. The obnoxious boss and the gossiping coworker: Yep, Jesus died for them. The killer and the rapist and the drug-dealer: He died for them. It upsets our spiritual applecart to think about unlovable others in this context. But I can find no spiritual loopholes that exclude certain people from Jesus's magnificent act of grace.

The apostle Paul explained the supernatural magnitude of God's actions on our behalf:

> We can understand someone dying for a person worth
> dying for, and we can understand how someone good
> and noble could inspire us to selfless sacrifice. But
> God put his love on the line for us by offering his
> Son in sacrificial death while we were of no use what-
> ever to him. (Romans 5:7-8)

Jesus's granting of salvation to the thief on the cross (see Luke 23:40-43) bothers many of us. We desire justice—most of the time. But when we are desperate for grace because we are facing justice, we might have a change in attitude.

God promises that justice is certain. *God* promises that. Not Congress or the local city council. *God* promises. My problem is that His time frame and mine tend to vary dramatically. I want justice now, but He metes out judgment when the time is right.

> God isn't late with his promise as some measure
> lateness. He is restraining himself on account of you,
> holding back the End because he doesn't want any-
> one lost. He's giving everyone space and time to
> change. (2 Peter 3:9)

I must learn to accept that God may grant room for repentance to those whom I wish would receive immediate judgment instead. And why wouldn't He? He did exactly the same thing for me.

2. Make Sure It Matters

Churches have split over the stupidest things imaginable. *Stupid* is a harsh and ugly word. But it fits. I would suggest that unless you are dividing over the core doctrinal truths of Christianity, then you are dividing in sin. To paraphrase comedian Jeff Foxwothy, if it ain't heresy, you just might be a Pharisee.

A recent case offers a concrete example of something worth fighting over. At considerable risk of offending some, I would suggest that the Episcopal Church's dispute over the ordination of V. Gene Robinson was a conflict of doctrinal integrity. Frankly, the intensity of the debate surprised me. Forgive me for being blunt, but Robinson did not meet the biblical mandate spelled out in 1 Timothy 3 to qualify for the position of elder, let alone bishop. We must defend the core doctrinal tenets, or the church will be tossed on every cultural wave that comes along. Robinson made a very troubling statement: "Just to say that it goes against tradition and the teaching of the church and Scripture does not necessarily make it wrong."[3] Oh really? If the teaching of Scripture is irrelevant, then what is to be our basis for distinguishing between right and wrong? What a dangerous argument to accept into the church.

Even if I were to agree with Robinson's argument, I would have to say that his actions did not demonstrate the sacrificial example of Jesus. Robinson chose to sow division in order to advance his own personal agenda. That sounds harsh, but it underscores a key issue in how the unchurched view us. If this relationship we claim to have with Jesus cannot generate peace inside the church, then what hope does it hold for those observing from afar? And what is our answer? I am a little tired of trotting out the lame bromide, "I'm not perfect; I'm just forgiven." As I have said many times, we have a responsibility to represent Christ, not self, when we take the title of Christian.

3. Use Your Mouth for Blessing

Have you seen the little book that details a multitude of uses for duct tape? I might suggest one more: If you have a critical spirit, tape your mouth shut. (I confess, that would reduce a fair amount of my own communication.) A bit of more scriptural but less colorful advice is contained in the book of James:

> It only takes a spark, remember, to set off a forest
> fire. A careless or wrongly placed word out of your
> mouth can do that. By our speech we can ruin the
> world, turn harmony to chaos, throw mud on a repu-
> tation, send the whole world up in smoke and go up
> in smoke with it, smoke right from the pit of hell.
> (James 3:5-6)

James didn't pull any punches, did he?

One good way to cling to unity is by not believing gossip about our fellow Christians. And we certainly shouldn't spread it any further. Gossip is a parasite that requires a host organism to survive; don't give gossip a place to live. Think of how many times you have believed something to be true only to find out that the information was mostly or even totally wrong. The threat of a libel or slander lawsuit causes some of us to be cautious in our written remarks about others. But we're not so careful when it comes to discussing our brothers and sisters in Christ. Are we really more concerned about the People's Court than the Kingdom's Court?

God has set some serious standards regarding how we communicate about others in the flock. Peter wrote:

> Be agreeable, be sympathetic, be loving, be compassionate, be humble. That goes for all of you, no exceptions. No retaliation. No sharp-tongued sarcasm. Instead, bless—that's your job, to bless. You'll be a blessing and also get a blessing. (1 Peter 3:8-9)

So there is an added bonus for your godly communication: a blessing at no extra charge.

On a personal note, thanks to all of you who have prayed for me concerning my sharp-tongued sarcasm. I certainly need the prayers—and you probably need the practice!

4. Remember the Greatest Commandment

Yes, love your neighbor as yourself. Some tough-to-love people plague our lives, don't they? I think God knew how difficult the task would be when He made that commandment a benchmark of walking with Him. Nothing I have encountered that is truly worthwhile is easy.

Marriage? Not easy, but definitely worth it. Parenting? Not easy, but certainly rewarding. Being a great athlete or student or musician? Not easy, but immensely satisfying. Why do we hope that the most incredible journey of our lives will be easy? Loving our neighbors across the board is humanly impossible; only by the grace of God and the moment-by-moment intervention of the Holy Spirit do we even stand a chance. (The difficulties of loving the unlovable, forgiving their offenses, and embracing our responsibilities to them as followers of Christ will be discussed in detail in chapter 10.)

5. Don't Leave Your Sense of Humor at the Altar

One of the reviews of *Bad Christians* described me as "flippant." To be honest I would have preferred "witty" or "erudite." Flippant! But the fact is that I believe a sense of humor is one of God's gifts to help get us to the finish line of life. "Humor is a rubber sword," observed Mary Hirsch. "It allows you to make a point without drawing blood."[4]

An examination of the life of Jesus seems to indicate that He possessed a sense of humor. God's writers did not set out to author a joke book, so you won't find the phrase *a Sadducee, a Pharisee, and a Roman walk into a bar* anywhere in the Bible. Still, you find glimpses of humor in the words of Jesus. For example, consider this exchange when the disciples came running up and asked Jesus the following question: "Did you know how upset the Pharisees were when they heard what you said?" (Matthew 15:12). I can see them looking at Jesus and waiting to hear Him say something like, "Really? I had better go get that straightened out. Those Pharisees are some important guys." I expect the Lord's answer first stunned and then amused them:

> Forget them. They are blind men leading blind men.
> When a blind man leads a blind man, they both end
> up in the ditch. (Matthew 15:14)

You will also note that Jesus was an oft-invited guest at weddings and banquets. His appearances, in fact, drew the ire of the Pharisees.

Think about it. If Jesus were a holier-than-thou, uptight, religious, suck-the-air-out-of-the-room sourpuss, would you want Him at your wedding party? Jesus must have been able to laugh and enjoy the common fellowship of others, and He was obviously a welcome and desired guest at the festivities. Let's join Jesus at Levi's dinner party, which was attended by some unsavory people, and see what happened:

> Levi gave a large dinner at his home for Jesus. Everybody was there, tax men and other disreputable characters as guests at the dinner. The Pharisees and their religion scholars came to his disciples greatly offended. "What is he doing eating and drinking with crooks and 'sinners'?"
>
> Jesus heard about it and spoke up, "Who needs a doctor: the healthy or the sick? I'm here inviting outsiders, not insiders—an invitation to a changed life, changed inside and out."
>
> They asked him, "John's disciples are well-known for keeping fasts and saying prayers. Also the Pharisees. But you seem to spend most of your time at parties. Why?"
>
> Jesus said, "When you're celebrating a wedding, you don't skimp on the cake and wine. You feast. Later you may need to pull in your belt, but this isn't the time. As long as the bride and groom are with you, you have a good time." (Luke 5:29-34)

At the risk of being flippant again, I'd like to point out that Jesus clearly knew how to party (in the good sense of the phrase). He knew how to interact warmly with others and connect with those around Him, no matter how unlike Him they might be.

The disciples whom Jesus assembled were a fascinating blend of common laborers and professional types. Imagine today if Christ went to the local pier to recruit some fishermen, dropped by the IRS to pick up a follower, then went over to the medical clinic, and so on. I would imagine this would be (at least initially) a fairly coarse group. I don't suspect, for instance, that the men dropped the earthy sense of humor they likely possessed when they dropped their nets to follow Jesus. Besides, part of any healthy and dynamic group relationship is having fun together. So I firmly believe there were times when Jesus and the Twelve told jokes and fish stories.

A lack of humor in the church apparently has been a problem for a while now. Teresa of Avila prayed this simple prayer in 1582: "From somber, serious, sullen saints, save us, O Lord." Amen, and amen.

There you have my little battle plan for unity: Remember that Christ died for everyone and not just your little holy huddle. If it is not heresy, it may not matter much. Use your mouth for blessing. Love your neighbor as yourself. And have a sense of humor.

Unintentional Wounds Hurt Too

In December 1979, a tragedy occurred in my home state of Ohio. The Who rock group came to Cincinnati to perform at Riverfront Stadium. The tickets were sold in a then-popular format called festival seating.

Ticket prices were fixed, and the best seats went to the concert-goers who could get inside most quickly. Needless to say, festival seating caused some chaos in the best of circumstances. But in Cincinnati that night, the self-centered desire for good seats led to disaster. When the doors finally opened, the impatient crowd surged forward, resulting in a crush of humanity. Eleven people were killed that night, and scores were injured.

I would venture that not a single person went to Riverfront Stadium that night with the intention of hurting (much less killing) another person. But hundreds of people were primarily concerned about their own interests: getting through the door first and securing a seat close to the stage. That seemingly harmless desire brought tragic results.

The same thing can easily happen in the body of Christ. We can get so focused on an agenda or goal that we don't realize we are spiritually wounding other sheep in the process. I would suggest that, more often than not, no one starts out with any intention of hurting another lamb. But while we are rounding up support to remove the pastor, some lambs are spiritually trampled and maybe even spiritually killed. They won't be back. Whenever we divide the church over an issue that is eternally inconsequential, some sheep will get crushed in the process. Such injuries are often faith-threatening.

As followers of Jesus we have to understand that our actions have consequences throughout the body of Christ—and throughout eternity. For the sake of the entire flock then, can we commit to praying before we speak, seeking counsel before we act, and even allowing situations other than "our will" to be done?

In His final hours, our Lord prayed primarily for our unity. I know that if someone I dearly loved made a dying request of me, I would do everything in my power to fulfill that desire. The Jesus who loved me enough to suffer the Cross made the dying request that I (and the rest of us in the church) demonstrate unity in order "to let the world know that you sent me and have loved them even as you have loved me" (John 17:23, NIV). Making an attempt at such unity certainly seems like the least we can do in gratitude for the unmerited gift of grace and salvation He has given to us. So let's make a commitment to fulfill Jesus's prayer and wish for us—out of love for Him, but also because unity can make a difference in our quest to restore at least some of our wounded lambs. It would be an excellent start.

— For Reflection and Discussion —

1. With all of the problems going on in Corinth, why do you think Paul addressed division first?

2. Read and meditate on Jesus's prayer in John 17. Why has the church historically had such a difficult time in coming "to complete unity" (verse 23, NIV)?

3. Does unity demand doctrinal conformity? Why or why not? What are the bottom-line absolutes of the Christian faith?

4. Review the five steps to unity suggested in this chapter. Does one in particular present a challenge to you? What can you do to improve in that area?

5. What will you do to help encourage greater unity in your church?

Chapter 4

THE HEART
OF A SHEPHERD

Serving Where We Are Called

After a big citywide revival had concluded, three pastors were discussing the results. The Methodist minister was delighted. "The revival was wonderful for us. We gained four new families." The Baptist minister chimed in, "We did even better! We have six new families!" The Presbyterian minister smiled and said, "Well, we did even better than that! We got rid of our ten biggest troublemakers."

Joke of the Day, MeMail.com, March 1, 2002

The word *pastor* comes from the Latin word for *shepherd*. Being the shepherd of one of God's flocks is an awesome and sobering responsibility. First of all, it is never easy to blend into a unified force for the Lord the eclectic group that the average church attracts. Paul explained to the early church the weightiness of a pastor's role:

Now it's up to you. Be on your toes—both for yourselves and your congregation of sheep. The Holy
Spirit has put you in charge of these people—God's
people they are—to guard and protect them. God
himself thought they were worth dying for. (Acts
20:28)

That is a responsibility to be taken quite seriously. The Holy
Spirit has put the shepherds in charge. Those of us who claim the
sacred title *Christian* must take very seriously our responsibility to
represent Christ with our lives. I believe our leaders are held to an
even higher level of prayerful responsibility even as they shepherd
their flocks.

I think that many of us read 1 Timothy and breathe a huge and
lengthy sigh of relief that these standards apply to "elders" only. How
about reading this passage in the context of any type of church leadership? The *New American Standard Bible, English Standard Version,*
and *New International Version* all use the term *overseer* instead of elder.
I view the standards as a benchmark for those who shepherd our
flocks.

If anyone wants to provide leadership in the church,
good! But there are preconditions: A leader must be
well-thought-of, committed to his wife, cool and
collected, accessible, and hospitable. He must know
what he's talking about, not be overfond of wine,
not pushy but gentle, not thin-skinned, not money-
hungry. He must handle his own affairs well, attentive
to his own children and having their respect. For if

someone is unable to handle his own affairs, how can
he take care of God's church? He must not be a new
believer, lest the position go to his head and the Devil
trip him up. Outsiders must think well of him, or
else the Devil will figure out a way to lure him into
his trap. (1 Timothy 3:1-7)

FOUR RESPECTFUL REQUESTS

I'll be the first to say, shepherd, that you do not have an easy job. I
know the flock often makes your life difficult, even impossible at
times. Many who are willing to cast stones at you could not begin to
carry the burden you handle every day. We often expect you to be a
spiritual superhero whom we can summon at will to save us from every
difficulty. We sometimes insist that you save our families at the expense
of your own. Please forgive our selfish and unrealistic demands.

That said, I hope you will understand that the requests and obser-
vations I am about to make are couched in deepest respect for what
you do and for what you sacrifice for us on a daily basis.

Request 1: Please Remember That There's No Business
Like Soul Business

We have been told that church is a business. Certainly many aspects of
the operation should be run in a professional manner. Such profes-
sionalism can mean the basic good stewardship of God's resources. No
argument there. And many principles followed by successful secular
companies can be applied to the practical function of our churches.
Successful businesses know, for example, that they must minimize
dissatisfied customers because unhappy consumers can damage a

company's reputation. Statistics show that disgruntled customers tell twenty times as many people about their negative experiences as contented folks tell about their good experiences. If we applied this probability to the church, we might gain some idea of how important it is to restore wounded lambs. (And, because spiritual issues are so emotionally charged, I suspect that disgruntled churchgoers might be even more vocal than consumers about their stories.) That volume of negative discussion hurts the cause of the church; we need to take responsibility for our part of the damage.

Still, there is some danger in viewing the church as a business. The church that flourished in the book of Acts was not run like a corporation. Listen to the description of that flourishing church:

> They committed themselves to the teaching of the apostles, the life together, the common meal, and the prayers.
>
> Everyone around was in awe—all those wonders and signs done through the apostles! And all the believers lived in a wonderful harmony, holding everything in common. They sold whatever they owned and pooled their resources so that each person's need was met. (Acts 2:42-45)

I know that such communal living is not likely to happen in America, but we can certainly come a little closer to the goal of "wonderful harmony." In a corporate environment, maintaining harmonious relationships among employees is not necessarily high on the list of priorities. But if unity is one of the church's critical goals, as was discussed in chapter 3, we'll have to abandon some business-minded ways of thinking and become more people-minded in our mode of operation. As I mentioned earlier, we don't have to be best buddies with everyone sitting in the pews, but we do have to be unified in the common cause of representing Christ to a declining culture.

I wrote at length about my vision for a sinner-sensitive church in *Bad Christians,* and I might have stumbled on a working model of that at The Haven in Euless, Texas. An associate pastor's wife read my book and contacted me to ask if I would consider speaking to the church. I was warned that their assembly was a bit "different." I visited the Web site and read the church slogan: "We love the hell out of people." I immediately e-mailed that I would come.

When I walked into the service, I was briefly taken aback. I had been told that this was "a biker church," and I was not quite sure how I—the suburban, middle-aged, khaki-wearing, polo-shirted guy—would fit in. Two things became immediately apparent. For one, this place was a hospital for sinners. Looking around the room, I saw people at every stage of the spiritual journey. Many faces showed signs of hard mileage in their lives. Some wore dress shirts and ties. Some wore T-shirts with slogans. Many were neatly coiffed. Many had long hair and ponytails. There was no shortage of tattoos and piercings. Black, white, Hispanic, and combinations of all of these had gathered together. I would venture that because of their living arrangements, their prior night's activities, or simply their appearance, many would have been unwelcome in other congregations (but thankfully not all). Remarkably, it was also apparent that everyone I met was clothed in the acceptance that should be found in any place that preaches the gospel of Jesus.

I couldn't help but think that this was how the New Testament church must have looked. I imagined groups of common laborers worshiping side-by-side with the wealthy elite in those early house churches. They were unlikely friends assembled to learn about the revolutionary teachings and grace of Jesus. The Haven offered me a picture of how the church described in the book of Acts functioned— before ZIP codes and suburban sprawl segregated us into homogeneous little holy huddles. Many of our churches are ecclesiastical versions of *The Stepford Wives.*

I probably don't need to tell you that the body of Christ at The Haven accepted my message with enthusiasm and love. The pastors at The Haven did not shrink from the truth but understood that God changes people in His sovereign timing and through His Word. I left that place thinking that I would much rather be with that body when Jesus returns than in some stodgy palatial church in a wealthy part of town.

So how do we create such an environment? Pastors who are more people-minded than business-minded can do a better job of caring for the flock in ways that please God. As Peter told the leaders of the church:

> Here's my concern: that you care for God's flock with
> all the diligence of a shepherd. Not because you have
> to, but because you want to please God. Not calculat-
> ing what you can get out of it, but acting sponta-
> neously. (1 Peter 5:2)

Request #2: Please Be Tender Toward Us Sinners

When Jesus appointed Peter as a shepherd of His lambs, He did not challenge Peter to gather large numbers of people into the "congregation." Christ did not ask Peter to build impressive structures to prove his love for Him. He didn't challenge Peter to build an organization that would impress the world. Here are the instructions that Jesus gave the apostle Peter:

> After breakfast, Jesus said to Simon Peter, "Simon, son of John, do you love me more than these?"
>
> "Yes, Master, you know I love you."
>
> Jesus said, "Feed my lambs."
>
> He then asked a second time, "Simon, son of John, do you love me?"
>
> "Yes, Master, you know I love you."
>
> Jesus said, "Shepherd my sheep."
>
> Then he said it a third time: "Simon, son of John, do you love me?"
>
> Peter was upset that he asked for the third time, "Do you love me?" so he answered, "Master, you know everything there is to know. You've got to know that I love you."
>
> Jesus said, "Feed my sheep." (John 21:15-17)

Jesus did not say, "Amuse my sheep." He did not say, "Entertain my sheep." He did not say, "Coddle my sheep with an easy path." And He certainly did not say, "Club my sheep when they cause trouble."

Some pastors and church leaders seem to believe that the best solution to solving problems among the body is to show "trouble-makers" the door. A pastor I greatly admire once told me, "That is why we have the exits clearly marked!" I chuckled and nodded my head because that is also my first response to difficult people. But, as I get older, I struggle with the bravado of that approach. Yeah, yeah, I know that some parishioners are nothing but trouble. But eliminating sheep as a growth strategy is a bit unsettling.

Paul reminds us that "God has carefully placed each part of the body right where he wanted it" (1 Corinthians 12:18). I would humbly ask leadership to prayerfully consider that God might have put even a troublemaker in the body for a reason. I listen to church leaders preach to struggling married couples, imploring them to trust God, stay together, and allow Christ who is living in them to work it out. Then I see that same leadership making only a token attempt to hold together difficult church relationships. The relationship of Christ to the church is likened to that between the groom and the bride. Can we preach such a high standard for relationships in marriage and then accept anything less from our shepherds?

Pastor David Hansen has listened to many "church-growth guns brag how after ten years of exponential growth in their church, virtually none of the original members were left." Pastor Hansen believes that biblical shepherding means figuring out how to include the challenging sheep in the life of the flock. He made a powerful and humble observation when he said, "Sometimes, when I complain that Mr. and Mrs. So-and-So are quenching the Spirit, what may really be happening is that they are quenching my ego."[1]

Peter did not advise the shepherd to show difficult rams and ewes the sheep gate so they could wander off to another flock. Instead, he charged shepherds with caring for the sheep in order "to please God" (1 Peter 5:2). Running off sheep may be the easiest thing to do. In some cases it may be the only thing you can do to save the flock. I know (and quoted in chapter 3) the scripture about warning the divisive person twice and then having nothing to do with him. But that admonition from Paul presumes a scriptural approach to church discipline and conflict resolution, an approach that seems to be in short supply in today's church culture. Discipline in the church should follow scriptural guidelines, and it must be done in love. Church discipline must never be used for retaliation, as tempting as that must be at times when a member of the flock gets ugly. Discipline that honors Christ builds up people; it does not punish and dismiss them.

I hope that any decision to ask a lamb to leave the flock would be prayerfully and painfully made. I pray that all shepherds will painstakingly follow biblical outlines for restoring that lamb to the flock. Some in the flock may make terrible choices. When you do discipline them, remember the words from Jude:

> Go after those who take the wrong way. Be tender
> with sinners, but not soft on sin. The sin itself stinks
> to high heaven. (Jude 23)

Please be tender with sinners. Jesus gave us an example of how to do this in His treatment of the woman caught in adultery. He was not "soft on sin," but He was breathtakingly tender in His treatment of her soul:

> Jesus stood up and spoke to her. "Woman, where are
> they? Does no one condemn you?"
> "No one, Master."
> "Neither do I," said Jesus. "Go on your way.
> From now on, don't sin." (John 8:10-11)

God Himself thought troublemakers were worth dying for. The easy sheep were worth dying for, but so were the difficult sheep. All are included in Christ's sacrifice.

Request #3: Please Take Seriously Your Responsibility to the Wounded Lamb

But many wounded lambs have not necessarily left the church because they were troublemakers or because they sinned or made bad choices. Many have been victims of wounds inflicted by the flock. Here I would offer the uncomfortable admonition to every shepherd to pray about your responsibility to the wounded lamb.

Joni and I have some experience regarding such wounds. Our third child, Katie, was born with a birth defect that resulted in a lack of brain development. She was not expected to live more than a few hours or days, at most, but she confounded the experts and lived for over a year. During that time, Katie became part of our busy family routine, going with us to ball games, various activities, and church. One Sunday morning we were blindsided by a phone call explaining that Katie would no longer be welcome in the church nursery. Apparently some of the other parents were, for various reasons, uncomfortable with her presence there.

When Joni and I suffered the heartbreak of our daughter's banishment from our church nursery (you can read the first part of Katie's story at www.daveburchett.com), we never heard from the shepherds of the church. The first and most obvious question is, Did they know? We learned later that some of the leaders were aware of and partly involved in the decision.

Would contact from the shepherds have helped Joni and me recover from the wound? Without question it would have helped to have heard that the leadership regretted, was saddened, or at least was aware that its decision had caused us pain. It would have been healing to know that our pastors had agonized (and prayed) over the decision to exclude our daughter from the church nursery. Would we have been restored to that flock? Perhaps. Certainly we would have had to work together to find a compromise on Katie's status in the nursery. But it is possible that a loving response from the shepherds could have returned us to the flock. I cannot give you a definitive or totally objective answer about that possibility. But I am confident that their reaching out to us would have helped.

I am sure that the situation regarding Katie put the shepherds of that church in an awkward position. Their nursery workers were uncomfortable with Katie's presence, and the shepherds had a responsibility to them. But by avoiding some uncomfortable communication with Joni and me, the leadership made the wound deeper than it ever needed to be. I don't want to come across as bitter, because God worked in amazing ways to honor Katie's life and heal our family. But I want to point out that avoiding an issue is not a biblical option for a shepherd. There is a saying that what you are afraid to do is a clear indicator of the next thing you need to do. Please pray for strength and grace to face the difficult conversations with members of your flock.

Request #4: Please Give Yourself and the Holy Spirit Some Credit

I would like to offer one more observation to church leaders. I am going to get myself in trouble again (thank God for my day job). But I wonder if your seminars for pastors focus a bit too much on how to increase the size and activity level of the flock instead of how to shepherd it.

May I suggest that God is big enough to be creative with His vision and purpose for your flock? When I study how God works throughout the Bible, I see that His methods are unique in almost every situation. I don't discount that much can be learned from other churches, but I do struggle with the "seminar mentality" that suggests it is important for Fellowship A to look as much as possible like Fellowship B because Fellowship B is, by all accounts, "successful." To draw a comparison, I cannot write like Philip Yancey because my brain isn't big enough. It would be a huge mistake for me to try to copy what Yancey does, and if I pursued that vain effort, I would miss God's purposes for me. So I attempt to communicate with some humor and candor what God is teaching *me.* I write like Dave Burchett, and I am confident that I will face little competition in this niche. What I'm trying to say is, give yourself and the Holy Spirit some credit. God may just have something in mind for your flock that won't come from any seminar.

By the way, I wonder what God's creation would have looked like if He'd done the work after a creation seminar. Every animal would probably look like a lion, an eagle, or a horse. But think of what we would miss. Don't the duckbill platypus and the pelican and the giraffe make life more interesting and fun?

Support Your Local Shepherd

Now to the creatures I am most comfortable with: my fellow sheep. Don't think I'm going to let you off the hook. Shepherds have an awesome responsibility for their flocks. But as I suggested in chapter 1, we have a serious responsibility too. We are all ambassadors of Christ, and this is a working appointment, not an honorary one. Paul wrote:

> We're Christ's representatives. God uses us to per-
> suade men and women to drop their differences and
> enter into God's work of making things right between
> them. (2 Corinthians 5:20)

Clearly, the conciliatory work—the tough job of achieving unity—does not belong to leadership alone. Besides working on getting along with our fellow sheep, we have responsibilities to our shepherds. The average pew-dweller is quick to criticize his or her pastor. I have had to confess and challenge that tendency in my own life. Being critical (and I know this will surprise you) comes naturally to me. Though it is a tad embarrassing to say so, I must inform you that the late children's television host Mr. Rogers taught me an amazing lesson about my own selfish and critical spirit.

Fred Rogers was an ordained Presbyterian minister, and he told this story of his time at Pittsburgh Theological Seminary. Each Sunday he would attend a different church in order to hear varying styles of preachers. One Sunday he heard a sermon that was, in Mr. Rogers's words, "The most poorly crafted sermon I had ever heard."

He turned to his friend to criticize the sad effort and found her in tears. "It was exactly what I needed to hear," she informed the stunned seminary student.

"That's when I realized," Rogers said, "that the space between someone doing the best he or she can and someone in need is holy ground. The Holy Spirit had transformed that feeble sermon for her—and, as it turned out, for me, too."

Allow me to humbly slip into my tennies and cardigan and confess that I have not had that attitude in my four decades or so of listening to sermons. How arrogant of me to expect a pastor always to address *my* needs whenever I grace the church with my presence. How self-centered I am to forget that God might ordain a message for just one person in the congregation whose immediate needs I cannot even begin to understand.

Again, this arrogant expectation is not new. The actions of self-centered and prideful folks who put themselves first have damaged God's flock for centuries. Listen to the words in Jeremiah:

> I had no idea what was going on—naive as a lamb
>> being led to slaughter!
> I didn't know they had it in for me,
>> didn't know of their behind-the-scenes plots:
> "Let's get rid of the preacher.
>> *That* will stop the sermons!
> Let's get rid of him for good.
>> He won't be remembered for long." (11:19)

God forbid that such a sinful plot should ever be uncovered in any church. Without question, a change in leadership is sometimes required. But it is never acceptable to make that change with a coup more befitting an oppressed nation than a house of worship. Our pastor-shepherds are human. Like us, they have weaknesses and failures. Yet they have taken the incredible and knee-buckling responsibility of being accountable to God. So we in the flock need to go through the biblical chain of authority, starting with long sessions of prayer, before we even consider running off a shepherd.

Furthermore, Paul instructed Timothy that we should appreciate and reward our leaders:

> Give a bonus to leaders who do a good job, especially
> the ones who work hard at preaching and teaching.
> Scripture tells us, "Don't muzzle a working ox," and,
> "A worker deserves his pay." (1 Timothy 5:17-18)

Perhaps quoting those verses will get me back in good stead with the pastors reading this book (despite the comparison to oxen). Paul added some advice about accusations against leaders:

> Don't listen to a complaint against a leader that isn't
> backed up by two or three responsible witnesses.
> (1 Timothy 5:19)

In the gospel of Matthew, Jesus Himself gave some direction about conflict resolution within the flock:

> If a fellow believer hurts you, go and tell him—work it
> out between the two of you. If he listens, you've made
> a friend. If he won't listen, take one or two others along
> so that the presence of witnesses will keep things hon-
> est, and try again. If he still won't listen, tell the church.
> If he won't listen to the church, you'll have to start over
> from scratch, confront him with the need for repen-
> tance, and offer again God's forgiving love. (18:15-17)

A shepherd being terrorized by sheep might be a humorous image if it weren't happening every day in our churches with tragic conse-quences. I believe we are entirely too nonchalant about personnel decisions that affect the body of believers that God has put together. I'm sorry, but I cannot put the replacement of a man or woman of God in the same category as changing the manager at a widget assembly plant.

GOT YOUR BACK, BROTHER!

In fact, rather than focus on how to replace a pastor, I think we can benefit by learning how to stand up for our leadership. I love the story of a teacher who was trying to make use of her self-esteem training. She started her class by saying, "If you think you're stupid, stand up!"

After a few seconds, a little boy stood up.

The teacher said, "Why do you think you're stupid, young man?"

"Oh, I don't think I'm stupid," he said. "I just hate to see you standing there all by yourself!"

Part of our responsibility to one another in the flock is to never leave a brother or sister or leader "standing there" all alone. We need to stand beside them.

One of the most touching moments in the groundbreaking career of Hall of Fame baseball player Jackie Robinson came from an unlikely source. As you likely know, Robinson was the first black baseball player in the major leagues. He endured hatred and incredibly abusive taunts from other players as well as fans. Pee Wee Reese was the team's starting shortstop, and his southern drawl might have led some to assume he was one of Robinson's enemies. They would have been wrong.

During infield practice prior to a game in Cincinnati, the rude remarks and gestures from the stands and the opponent's dugout escalated in ugliness. The greatly respected Reese made a point to walk from his position at shortstop to his teammate at second base. Reese faced the crowd and the Reds' dugout, put his arm around his teammate, and simply talked to him as he would to any other Dodger player. He didn't care that Robinson's skin color was different. He was Reese's teammate, and he deserved Reese's support. Robinson said later that he "never felt alone on the ball field after that day." The diminutive Reese stemmed a rising tide of hatred with a simple act of grace and love.

We need a lot of Pee Wee Reeses in the church. The body of Christ needs people who have the grace to set aside differences, disagreements, and prejudices, and put an arm around their teammate, whether pastor or elder or fellow member, no matter how much they might disagree on the unconventional service start time.

Although I am not a pastor, I pray that God will give me a shepherd's heart. I pray that He will teach me to care about every lamb He has placed in my little flock of influence. Paul acknowledged this need for Christian community in his letter to the church at Rome:

> Laugh with your happy friends when they're happy;
> share tears when they're down. Get along with each
> other; don't be stuck-up. Make friends with nobodies;
> don't be the great somebody. Don't hit back; discover
> beauty in everyone. If you've got it in you, get along
> with everybody. (Romans 12:15-18)

Interested in a church like that? That question should rank right up there with brilliant queries like, "Do you want a million dollars?" Such a church is possible only if we are willing to do what the Lord asks of us.

Do everything readily and cheerfully—no bickering, no second-guessing allowed! Go out into the world uncorrupted, a breath of fresh air in this squalid and polluted society. Provide people with a glimpse of good living and of the living God. (Philippians 2:14-15)

WHAT ARE WE REFLECTING?

When I talk to my unchurched friends about Christianity, they rarely say we are a breath of fresh air and a glimpse of the living God. Though we attend seminars about evangelism, we're not very good at showing the world what it looks like to allow Christ to live through us. If we could show this "squalid and polluted society" that kind of lifestyle, our evangelism efforts would be much better received. In fact, if our lives showed that we are truly sold out to the teachings of Jesus, we probably wouldn't need much more than an ability to explain salvation in order to bring others to Christ.

To the church at Ephesus Paul wrote:

I want you to get out there and walk—better yet, run!—on the road God called you to travel. I don't want any of you sitting around on your hands. I don't want anyone strolling off, down some path that goes nowhere. And mark that you do this with humility and discipline—not in fits and starts, but steadily, pouring yourselves out for each other in acts of love, alert at noticing differences and quick at mending fences.

> You were all called to travel on the same road and
> in the same direction, so stay together, both outwardly
> and inwardly. (Ephesians 4:1-4)

All of us are indeed called to travel down the same road. And do we ever need to be going in the same direction! Samuel Johnson wrote that "God does not propose to judge a man until his life is over. Why should you and I?" That is a great question. I am a vastly different man at fifty than I was at thirty. I hope I will continue to grow in faith as the years go by. I will confess that I had only passing concern for my fellow members of my flock. Now I see the tragic loss and damage to the kingdom of God by allowing so many of His sheep to wander away. I would challenge you to consider your role in restoring our legions of lost and wounded lambs.

So I hope you will join me in asking God to give you a shepherd's heart. No doubt about it, there are some ugly and humanly unlovable sheep in the flock. But listen to these words from Paul:

> May our dependably steady and warmly personal God
> develop maturity in you so that you get along with
> each other as well as Jesus gets along with us all. Then
> we'll be a choir—not our voices only, but our very
> lives singing in harmony in a stunning anthem to the
> God and Father of our Master Jesus! (Romans 15:5-6)

Close your eyes and imagine for a moment the body of Christ singing in harmony. Is it even possible? Only if each of us prays for a shepherd's heart. That kind of heart is available…if we want it.

— For Reflection and Discussion —

1. What are some of the expectations you have for the pastor of your church?

2. What dangers do you see in running a church like a business?

3. Has any church you've been part of been too quick to dismiss those who cause problems or make mistakes (either in leadership or not)? In such cases, what should be the church's response? Why?

4. What is your typical attitude toward your pastor's sermons? Does this attitude need to change? Ask God to reveal something to your heart this week during the sermon that will draw you closer to Him.

5. What responsibilities do you have to minister to your shepherd? Write down one way in which you can do this and look for an opportunity to reach out in the coming week.

6. Read Romans 12, then list some characteristics of a healthy Christian community. How well does your church compare (be specific)? What could you do—no matter how small—to help bring your church closer to Paul's vision?

7. Ask God to reveal someone whom you need to pray for because of your unloving attitude toward him or her. Pray for this person each day and ask Jesus to change your heart.

Chapter 5

NEVER LEAVE A LAMB BEHIND!

Mobilizing a Search-and-Rescue Team

Too many people don't care what happens as long as it doesn't happen to them.

WILLIAM HOWARD TAFT

When I learned that author Mike Yaconelli had died as a result of an automobile accident, I was deeply saddened. Mike was a kindred spirit in his love for and ministry to wounded and abandoned lambs. A founding editor of the irreverent magazine *The Door*, he had recently written a wonderful book called *Messy Spirituality*. We had struck up an e-mail friendship, and Mike had invited me to join him on his boat in San Diego the next time I went to the West Coast. We had agreed to follow the advice offered in 1 Timothy 5:23 while we discussed our walk with Jesus.

I regret that I will have to postpone that discussion until I meet Mike in heaven. But I will always be grateful for what he taught me about being honest in my Christian experience. In a 1995 interview, Mike told the *Mars Hill Review:* "People want to have a faith, but they are tired of lying. People are tired of pretending their lives are better than they actually are." Later he noted that "we are told that when Jesus comes into your life he takes all the disparities, all the odd ups-and-downs of life, all of your struggles, and gives you balance. That's baloney—it's a lie. I think Jesus makes our lives lopsided and crazy." Mike was so right. Jesus turns our little cultural applecarts upside down, and that is what makes our faith walk so very interesting. Mike also said that he was "convinced that people are looking for something that says, 'You're not alone, you are loved in spite of the flaws and the junk in your life.' People want to know that there is hope out there and that some sense can be made of life. That their small life with its little bit of everydayness can actually make a difference and have a kind of power and authority."[1]

No one communicated that the lambs of Jesus are loved in spite of their flaws better than Mike Yaconelli. Unfortunately, many of us are far less articulate on that point. Consider this honest evaluation of the church from the always articulate George Barna. It is both convicting and challenging.

> Regardless of its true character and intent, the Christian community is not known for love, nor for a life transforming faith. Outdated means of outreach, inappropriate assumptions about people's faith, and a lack of passion for helping non-believers to receive God's love and acceptance are hindering the Church from fulfilling its mandate. America remains one of

the largest mission fields in the world, and the American Church remains the most richly endowed body of believers on the planet. There is no lack of potential.[2]

Barna is painfully correct. And I am convinced that another big hindrance to the church's fulfillment of its mandate is the legion of wounded and abandoned lambs. We do not have the benefit of their talents and fellowship. And a more subtle danger is that they, in their pain, are probably leading others away from our flocks.

When you encounter unchurched folks, mention Christianity and see what stories you hear. I was stunned by how many people volunteered an account of their own woundedness when they heard that I had written *Bad Christians.* Just by using the anecdotal material I receive from readers, I could write a whole series of *Bad Christian* books (don't worry, I won't). The pain of wounded lambs will naturally influence those around them. Go to a search engine and type in something like "ex-Christians." You will be amazed and heartbroken by what you find. Hundreds of angry and wounded lambs are pouring out their anguish to an audience that generally reinforces what they feel. Instead they need to hear from their former flock that we care, we miss them, we need them, and we want them to come back.

Operation "Bring 'Em Back Alive"

Earlier in this book I mentioned the concept of reevangelism. To reiterate, I am not suggesting that those who leave the church have lost their salvation and must be brought back to the saving knowledge of

Jesus. Instead I am talking about *restoring* to the flock the millions who have dropped out of the church because they have been wounded, neglected, or both.

I want to be an instrument in restoring some of those wandering and wounded lambs to the flock. I hope to enlist you in the cause. It is not easy to be a part of the search-and-rescue team for the Lord's missing sheep. It takes, among other things, a patient and loving spirit. This chapter will outline my personal vision for a search-and-rescue team that I believe all Christians can make a part of their corporate and personal ministry.

The psalmist pleaded, "Should I wander off like a lost sheep—seek me!" (Psalm 119:176). I am confident that many caring sheep in the flock desire to do just that. The challenge is in how we can accomplish that goal.

COUNTING SHEEP

In order to seek something that is lost, you must first notice that it is missing. (You don't get this kind of insight everywhere!) It would have been easy to note missing sheep in the church where I grew up. If the seats near the aisle in the third pew of the right section were empty, you would have known that the Johnsons were absent. This is not the case in today's church. Our whirlwind lifestyle and sporadic church attendance make it really difficult to track the sheep. My idea to outfit church members with an electronic tracking device would probably meet resistance. (I can see it now: "We have a missing lamb on a golf course in Altoona... A rescue unit is on the way.") So I have come up with a few alternatives.

1. Create a Culture in Which Seeking and Healing the Wounded and Abandoned Is a Priority

The first item on my wish list is shepherds who emphasize, through sermons and other regular church communications, that every lamb matters. Also, everyone in the church could participate in prayer groups that regularly pray for the church's wounded, lost, and abandoned. It can be enormously comforting to know that a group of Christians is praying for your welfare. I would love to see churches establish regular classes and/or healing seminars for those wounded by the church. I think that many injured lambs feel alone, and having a forum where they can express their hurt and share their concerns with others would be therapeutic. Regular off-campus gatherings for honest discussion of difficult topics of faith could be a good reentry point for many wounded lambs.

2. Designate and Train "Helper Shepherds" Within the Church

When I consider the difficulty of keeping track of my own family members, I shudder at the thought of being responsible for two hundred or five hundred or five thousand people. I mentioned in chapter 1 that we (the sheep) need to assume the role of small-flock shepherds to aid our leaders. And I believe that we regularly need to count the sheep in our small-group flock and take responsibility for them.

In my search-and-rescue model, this ideal culture that values seeking the wounded would not be possible without the assistance of small-flock "Helper Shepherds." It would be each Helper Shepherd's responsibility to monitor the sheep in his or her small group of ten to fifteen people. When a person or family is absent, the Helper Shepherd would be the first to make sure the church attempts to seek the missing sheep. A phone call or note might reveal that illness or a weekend trip kept that person away. Immediately noticing someone's absence will make real to that person the caring nature of the church. And it will help us avoid the often innocent mistake of assuming everything is okay. A lamb whose absence is not noticed right away can soon fall victim to the "out of sight, out of mind" syndrome. Having Helper Shepherds in place will, at the very least, let missing lambs know they are missed and valued. John S. Savage of L.E.A.D. Consultants, Inc., has determined that immediate response to an angry and wounded lamb could recover up to 80 percent of the injured sheep! His research reveals that after six to eight weeks, a wounded person psychologically seals off the pain and is much more difficult to restore.[3]

Also, by the time most churches discover they have an angry or wounded lamb among them (or running away from them), other incidents will have likely disguised the original wound. Getting wounded lambs to tell their stories sooner rather than later will make it easier to address the real reason for the pain, which will greatly increase the lambs' chances of healing and returning to the flock.

3. Encourage Communication with Leadership

Many times the pastor or other church leaders simply do not realize that a member of the flock is struggling or hurt. When an absent lamb needs prayer, the Helper Shepherd can let key ministers in the body know. Perhaps, with the lamb's permission, the Helper could fill out a prayer card explaining why the person is gone (death in family, illness, tough period at work, and so on). In cases where the person has left because of a wounding, the Helper Shepherd could share this confidentially with the leadership (also with the permission of the lamb). No gossip is needed here. But if ministers had an opportunity to take healing action quickly, perhaps fewer sheep would be lost.

Sometimes wounded lambs might share a hurt with a member of the flock that they would not reveal to leadership—even to Helper Shepherds. Church members who know that their church cares about these wounded lambs also need a way to communicate with key ministers (again with the wounded lamb's permission). Publishing leaders' e-mail addresses and phone numbers or establishing private Web links to the pastor in charge of the search-and-rescue ministry can facilitate accessibility to people who can help.

Finally, make the communication two-way. A Helper Shepherd could send a letter to the wounded lamb when he or she notices the absence of the lamb. Many churches do this already, but rarely does the letter address the missing person's situation. A personalized letter from the pastor based on the input of the Helper Shepherd might even better demonstrate the church's genuine concern.

4. Offer Electronic Connections

I have found that wounded lambs are willing to communicate with anyone who cares about their hurt. Hundreds of people who don't even know what I look like have e-mailed me to describe the pain of their church experience. They perceived that I cared, and any response from me seemed to help. Perhaps an e-mail ministry to share concerns and hurts could be established in the church. I realize that some might not trust the shepherds enough to be vulnerable, but most people simply want to be heard by somebody. Certainly some needs are too complicated to address via e-mail, but that very invitation could open a door and encourage an injured sheep to seek counseling. Internet-savvy churches might create a forum or monitored (to prevent gossip and slander) chat room where people could discuss their concerns. Perhaps setting up a system that offered anonymity might encourage the wounded lamb to take the first step. For example, allowing church-goers to sign in with a user name instead of their real name might offer a safe haven for beginning restoration.

5. Be Honest About the Church

When speaking with the wounded, don't promise something that the church can't deliver in the hopes of luring them back. For example, if your church is going through a conflict, don't promise that it will never happen again. George Barna's research found that 70 percent of churchgoers avoid conflict whenever possible. Is it any wonder that conflict in the church sends the sheep scattering to the hills? So, instead, try to focus on the healing the Good Shepherd offers. Chapters 1 and 3 might help you address the church shortfall when it comes to church unity.

6. Pursue to the Best of Your Ability Reconciliation Between Shepherd and Sheep

When a wounded lamb feels as if a shepherd has wounded him or her, I would hope that the leader would desire to seek forgiveness, repair the damage, and if possible, reconcile. (I will cover those topics in much more detail in chapter 9.) The response of the lamb is not the issue. The shepherd's willingness to try to reconcile is critical to the health of the flock. As I mentioned in chapter 4, the bottom line is that we expect more of our shepherds—and so does God.

I would also encourage leaders to try to find out why sheep leave their flock. It may not always be possible to survey those who leave the church, but feedback from them can be invaluable. In fact, the data can serve as an early warning system for problems emerging in the body. During the Iraq war our troops used chickens as a part of their defense strategy. The soldiers had actual clucking chickens with their platoons. It seems that these feathered friends are far more sensitive to airborne chemical agents, and distressed chickens served as an early warning sign that the troops needed to don gas masks. Likewise, wounded lambs leaving the flock can be an early warning sign that certain issues need to be addressed in the church.

Obviously, asking people why they've left a church is a touchy issue. Pastor and church-growth expert Lyle Pointer has compiled an excellent list of issues to consider and questions to ask those who leave the church.[4] Applying his strategy, I have compiled the following list of considerations and questions for a church leader to ponder before such a meeting:

- Ask the Lord to help you leave your pride behind. You may hear some things that you will want to refute. Don't.
- Realize that wounded and probably angry lambs are likely to be defensive. Let them know you want to hear their input. Your only goals are to make sure they know the church has not forgotten them and to improve the ministry of the church by hearing their honest critique.
- Assure them that you are there only to listen, not to argue or dismiss their opinion.
- Ask them what first attracted them to the church.
- Ask them if a disappointment with the church caused them to leave (or consider leaving) the flock.
- If so, find out if there is anything you can do as leadership to help resolve the anger or hurt.

- Ask what one thing about the church they would change if they were in charge.
- As you listen, and if the situation calls for it, seek opportunities to ask the wounded lambs to forgive you and/or the body for their injuries.
- Tell them they are valued and missed. Tell them they will be welcomed back if there is a chance of reconciliation.
- When you leave, pray with the wounded lambs and ask God to bless them no matter what they decide.
- Follow up to make sure they get settled into a church, even if it's not yours. If they do not, continue to gently encourage them to return to your church flock or to find a new flock. Do whatever is in your ability not to lose touch with them.

SERVANTHOOD ENHANCERS

No doubt about it: Tending to the needs of a wounded lamb can be emotionally and physically exhausting, especially if the wounds are chronic. Pastor Mathew Woodley notes that although their wounds are very real, these wounded lambs often develop a suffocating and ultimately self-defeating dependence on a pastor or other member of the flock. Overtly or innocently, wounded lambs can take all the time you will give. They are hurting, and you offer hope to relieve their pain. So Pastor Woodley suggests that search-and-rescuers communicate clear boundaries. For example, he generally restricts calls from his chronically wounded lambs to the office, where he can give them his full attention.

Pastor Woodley made the following convicting comments that I will simply present here since I am smart enough not to touch up a Michelangelo:

> I gravitate toward people who will make me look and
> feel successful about my ministry. The chronically
> wounded usually don't qualify as success-enhancers.
> They do, however, qualify as servanthood-enhancers.
> CWNs [the Chronically Wounded and Needy] have
> taught me a profound lesson: servanthood, not suc-
> cess, is my calling. Success is about me, my need
> for approval and control; servanthood is about God,
> my heart's longing to glorify Him. So pastoring the
> deeply wounded is actually a gift. Slowly, painfully, I
> relinquish my unholy hankering for success. Then, as
> Jesus calls me into the freedom of servanthood, I can
> wait quietly for the Holy Spirit to heal in His way
> and in His timing.[5]

I so wish I had written that.

With Friends Like These, Who Needs Enemies?

God gave us a powerful illustration in the book of Job of how *not* to help restore a wounded sheep. I would like to give special thanks to our friends Eliphaz from Teman, Bildad from Shuhah, and, of course, Zophar from Naamath. If you don't recognize the names, these were Job's buddies, who founded the original seminar on how *not* to deal with a wounded lamb. Let's look at the applications for us.

Do Not Assume That Wounded Lambs Are at Fault for Their Difficulties

Our first instructor is Eliphaz from Teman who told the suffering Job:

> Think! Has a truly innocent person ever ended up
>> on the scrap heap?
>> Do genuinely upright people ever lose out in
>> the end?
> It's my observation that those who plow evil and
>> sow trouble reap evil and trouble. (Job 4:7-8)

Do not assume they are at fault, and do not assume they are *not* at fault. Allow God to make that verdict. Eliphaz arrogantly proclaimed that it was his "observation" that you reap what you sow. That principle is often true, but we know from God's Word that Job's trials were unrelated to his spiritual condition. Thinking he knew the facts, Eliphaz jumped to an incorrect and hurtful conclusion.

Learn from Eliphaz and listen without judgment. Allow wounded lambs to express their frustration and pain—something that goes against every natural instinct most of us possess. As for me, I usually want to jump in and fix the problem. But God is teaching me to listen, pray, and allow the Holy Spirit to direct my words and actions.

Further, chastising a wounded lamb for missing church is not a loving approach. Perhaps you can talk with the person outside the church over a cup of coffee. Giving them your time says, "You are important to me." When you meet with a wounded lamb, I would suggest using any one of the following three strategies: (1) Be empathetic and listen, (2) Be empathetic and listen, and (3) Be empathetic and listen. I devised these strategies specifically for me because my previous program consisted of only one strategy: (1) Listen impatiently, address their problem with some vaguely appropriate Bible verses, and then dramatically share my own personal horror story that far exceeds their puny little problem. I can assure you there is not a book—nor a rescued lamb—in my previous strategy.

Focus on Being Empathetic
Our next lesson also comes from Eliphaz:

> So, what a blessing when God steps in and corrects
> you! (Job 5:17)

I am pretty sure that Job was not at the "I'm thinkin' what a blessing this is" phase of his ordeal. Though he remained faithful to the Lord and did not sin against Him, Job was angry, frustrated, bitter, bewildered, and downcast about all the loss he was suffering. In other words, Job was human. His trust in God was supernatural; his rollercoaster ride of emotions was normal.

The truth that God can use every circumstance for ultimate good is a foundational promise of our faith. However, it is often difficult, if not impossible, to understand that truth during the turbulence of the trial. When I am on a plane, I know intellectually that those big bumps and shudders are caused by disturbances in the air and that I will surely survive them. But I just want to get through the turbulence and back to smooth air. It's much easier to think clearly about the aerodynamics of turbulence in peace.

Thus, simple phrases like, "I'm sorry" or "That must have hurt," can create lifesaving connections with a wounded lamb. You don't need to offer answers or try to explain things that are often without explanation on this side of hindsight.

It's More Productive to Help Wounded Lambs Deal with Anger and Hurt Than to Assign Blame

Bildad from Shuhah was next to speak at our What Not to Do seminar:

> It's plain that your children sinned against him—
>> otherwise, why would God have punished them?
>> (Job 8:4)

Insight like Bildad's just isn't real helpful, is it? If you remember the story, Job's children were killed in a storm. What a dangerous (and, we find out later, evil) thing to say to a wounded child of God. And talk about pouring rock salt in a gaping emotional wound. Job's children were dead! This verse reminds me of when Joni and I were informed by one church person that sin in our lives had no doubt led to our daughter Katie's terminal birth defect.

Jesus made it clear that there is no direct connection between trouble in this life and a person's sin tally. I will cover this in more detail in chapter 8, but for now, let's simply agree that it's more productive to help wounded lambs deal with their anger and hurt than to assign blame. Blame should come only from the One able to ascertain where it should fall.

While we are on the subject of assigning blame, however, I am compelled to touch on a delicate issue that is troubling for many today: emotional and physiological struggles that some Christians believe are always and "plainly" spiritual matters. Psychiatrist Dwight L. Carlson noted that up to 15 percent of the American population struggles with significant emotional problems. Is it illogical that at least some percentage of our flock also suffers from such problems? He wrote, "For them our churches need to be sanctuaries of healing, not places where they must hide their wounds."[6] Many of us freely seek prayer for our malfunctioning body parts, but we dare not ask for prayer for our depression or emotional problems. There is simply too great a stigma attached.

Famous evangelist and preacher Charles Spurgeon struggled so much with depression that he was sometimes absent from the pulpit for two to three months a year. Upon returning from one absence, he confessed to his congregation:

> I was lying upon my couch during this last week, and my spirits were sunken so low that I could weep by the hour like a child, and yet I knew not what I wept for—but a very slight thing will move me to tears just now—and a kind friend was telling me of some poor old soul living near, who was suffering very great pain, and yet she was full of joy and rejoicing. I was so distressed by the hearing of that story, and felt so ashamed of myself, that I did not know what to do; wondering why I should be in such a state as this; while this poor woman, who had a terrible cancer, and was in the most frightful agony,

could nevertheless "rejoice with joy unspeakable, and full of glory."[7]

Like the apostle Paul, Spurgeon came to realize the shepherding value of his affliction. "I would go into the deeps a hundred times to cheer a downcast spirit. It is good for me to have been afflicted, that I might know how to speak a word in season to one that is weary."[8]

Brain-chemistry imbalances also fall into this category of painful struggle. I was diagnosed as an adult with Attention Deficit Disorder. Some think that is not a valid diagnosis but merely a faddish disorder. But understanding how my brain works has helped me function better in my job and my relationships. Learning about ADD has also given me the freedom to try some medications that increase the levels of serotonin in my brain and moderate the emotional swings and difficulties in focusing that are common to that disorder. I have been taking an SRI medication for about five years, and it has made an incredible difference in my life. I would venture to say that my writing career would likely not have developed had God not revealed to me this knowledge and the subsequent remedy.

All that to say this: Some of what I once considered a spiritual problem I have come to realize was actually a physiological imbalance. And before you send that e-mail condemning me for taking medications (which is clear evidence of my lack of faith), I would point out that a drug that regulates the chemical balance in the brain is absolutely no different from a drug that controls sugar levels for diabetics or regulates blood pressure for heart patients. It would be hurtful for anyone to suggest that your arthritis pain is merely a lack of faith. You might be angry if someone told you that a spiritual problem was causing you to suffer acid reflux and heartburn. We need to get past this wrong idea that a Christian cannot take a medication for depression or emotional issues. We should look for spiritual issues where they exist, for physiological and emotional issues where they exist, and for Christ's healing for all of that.

The bottom line: In a search-and-rescue ministry we must not shovel blame or guilt onto the sheep experiencing these problems, especially when they're trying to do something about them.

Don't Kick 'Em When They're Down

Back to Job. Welcome, Zophar from Naamath, to our discussion:

> How I wish God would give you a piece of his mind,
> tell you what's what!
> I wish he'd show you how wisdom looks from
> the inside,
> for true wisdom is mostly "inside."
> But you can be sure of this,
> you haven't gotten half of what you deserve.
> (Job 11:5-6)

Can you imagine what Job must have thought about this line of reasoning? He had lost *everything,* including his health. What more could possibly go wrong? Death, as Job repeatedly noted, would have been a blessed relief.

I cannot emphasize it enough: Leave the judgment robes at home when you speak to wounded lambs. The goal of the search-and-rescuer is to engage, listen, comfort, restore, and return them to the loving embrace of the Good Shepherd.

It is worth noting that the first round of "help" from his friends generated this cynical response from Job:

> I'm sure you speak for all the experts,
>> and when you die there'll be no one left
>>> to tell us how to live.

(I must make a note to thank Job for preceding me in the ministry of sarcasm. But I digress.)

> But don't forget that I also have a brain—
>> I don't intend to play second fiddle to you.
>> It doesn't take an expert to know these
>>> things.
>
> I'm ridiculed by my friends:
>> "So that's the man who had conversations
>>> with God!"
> Ridiculed without mercy:
>> "Look at the man who never did wrong!"
>
> It's easy for the well-to-do to point their fingers
>> in blame,
>> for the well-fixed to pour scorn on the strugglers.
>>> (Job 12:2-5)

Clearly, the judgment of Job's "friends" only added to his hurt. It is indeed easy to point fingers when someone else is going through difficulty. I pray that we will show grace to the wounded lambs. First, because they need it, but more selfishly, because we soon may need that grace returned.

Global Perspective Does Not Help Lessen the Pain of a Raw Wound

Eliphaz of Teman spoke a second time. (I'm sure that excited Job.)

> Do you think you're the first person to have to deal
> with these things? (Job 15:7)

Most of us know that we are not the first to have these problems and that we are probably not the worst case on the docket of world problems. See "Focus on Being Empathetic" on page 101.

Remember That a Wounded Lamb's Pain Is Not About You

Zophar from Naamath again took his turn. Sigh.

> I can't believe what I'm hearing!
>> You've put my teeth on edge, my stomach
>>> in a knot.
> How dare you insult my intelligence like this!
>> Well, here's a piece of my mind! (Job 20:2-3)

On this second round, Zophar took the seminar to a new level. Now Job's problems were all about *him!* "You put *me* on edge, tied *my* stomach in a knot, and insulted *my* intelligence." Then he gave Job a piece of his mind that he likely couldn't spare. When you minister to wounded lambs, please remember: Their pain is not about you.

You are a representative of the Good Shepherd, and your mission is to restore the injured lambs to the flock.

COMFORT VERSUS CORRECTION

Job had more to say about the ineffectiveness of his friends:

> I've had all I can take of your talk.
> What a bunch of miserable comforters! (Job 16:2)

It seems rather obvious that Job was looking for comfort and not theological "insight" and debate. He had already decided to hold steadfast to God.

Through all his trials, Job did not turn on God (see Job 2:10), but a careful reading of the rest of Job's story shows that he was extremely candid with God about his feelings. I think that we fear being honest with God, as if He doesn't already know our feelings. Another role of the search-and-rescue team is to encourage that honest, gut-level communication with God. Expressing such emotions can begin the healing process.

In recent years I have discovered how valuable it is to write and see on paper my feelings and frustrations. If you thought *Bad Christians* was a bit edgy, you should have seen the first draft! Some of the feelings that poured out as I wrote were anything but edifying. They exposed emotions and issues that I needed to address with God. It was quite helpful (and a bit unsettling) to see those things on paper. But it was instrumental in allowing me to deal with them.

Also, Job's lament to his friends gives us another clue about the heart of the hurting sheep. He felt betrayed and could not understand how his friends could accuse him when he only needed their support.

> Time after time after time you jump all over me.
>> Do you have no conscience, abusing me like
>>> this?...
> Why do you insist on putting me down,
>> using my troubles as a stick to beat me?...
> Look at me—I shout "Murder!" and I'm ignored;
>> I call for help and no one bothers to stop.
>>> (Job 19:3,5,7)

Understand that the pain is multiplied when wounded lambs feel that the church ignored or attacked them when they were already down. Wounded lambs will say some outlandish things that you might feel the urge to refute. Again, I caution you to not jump too quickly to "correct" wounded lambs who says things that are bitter, ugly, and over the top. Often they merely need to vent and are only seeking a safe place to do so. If their venting becomes a personal attack, you might gently steer them back toward the real issues. But at this stage be cautious about making the anger into a "spiritual" shortcoming. Again, I offer Job's pals as an example of what not to do. First, Job made the kind of statement that a wounded lamb might throw out there in frustration.

> Believe me, I'm blameless.
>> I don't understand what's going on.
>> I hate my life! (Job 9:21)

My first reaction would be to argue, "You can't really *hate* your life. Don't you know that you have so much to be thankful for? Blah, blah, blah." Certainly, introduce some of the positives that might be evident in the situation. But when a person is pouring out anger and hurt, don't race to point out how "wrong" his or her perspective might be.

From my experience, wounded lambs are best served by the following messages:

- I care about you.
- I will do whatever I can for you.
- I will be here if you need me.
- I promise to pray for you.

Later, the Bible details an amazing exchange between Job and God that delves into the eternal question of suffering and the sovereignty of God. I find it telling that after that conversation the Lord did not let Job's friends slither away without censure.

> After GOD had finished addressing Job, he turned
> to Eliphaz the Temanite and said, "I've had it with
> you and your two friends. I'm fed up! You haven't
> been honest either with me or about me—not the
> way my friend Job has. So here's what you must
> do. Take seven bulls and seven rams, and go to
> my friend Job. Sacrifice a burnt offering on your
> own behalf. My friend Job will pray for you, and
> I will accept his prayer. He will ask me not to treat
> you as you deserve for talking nonsense about me,
> and for not being honest with me, as he has."
> (Job 42:7-8)

God was not at all pleased with the mistreatment of His servant. His words offer a sobering and convicting lesson about our responsibility to deal faithfully, honestly, and tenderly with wounded brothers and sisters. God clearly takes note of how we deal with His lambs.

WORTH THE RISK

As I said before, not all lost and wandering sheep will return. As Pastor Woodley noted, "Ministering to CWNs [Chronically Wounded and Needy] involves an openness to failure." But I am going to challenge you to focus on the mutual joy that even one successful rescue can generate. Perhaps we might adopt the attitude of a major league baseball player.

I suspect that baseball players deal with more professional failure than any other athlete. A superstar baseball player fails seven out of ten times at bat. I am writing this chapter in Seattle, where the Texas Rangers designated hitter Rafael Palmeiro just struggled through a tough night. Rafi made three unimpressive outs in his first three times at bat. But the fourth time at bat, he blasted a three-run homer that tied the game and helped the Rangers win. No doubt our search-and-rescue success ratio might mirror Palmeiro's results:

Failure.

Failure.

Failure.

Success and joy!

Is it worth the multiple failures to get to that fourth at-bat? I think that Rafael Palmeiro and his team would quickly say, "Yes!" And I think the risk-reward ratio of our wounded-lamb search-and-rescue mission is also worth the effort.

We have God-given responsibility to care. We need to have a plan to identify the wounded and missing sheep. And then it is time to mount a search-and-rescue campaign.

The next section is written for the wounded lambs. Perhaps you who desire to do search-and-rescue will find insight into their plight helpful to your own efforts.

— For Reflection and Discussion —

1. Why do people leave the church?
2. Why is it so tough to minister to and love some wounded lambs? Do you believe the investment of time and energy is worth it? Explain.
3. Reread the section about Job's friends. What lesson about what not to do sticks out for you?
4. What can the church do to better deal with people struggling with difficult emotional or physiological issues?
5. What is the corporate responsibility of the church to seek the Lord's lost and wounded sheep? What does the church risk losing when it abdicates this responsibility?
6. What are some ways in which individuals can be involved in bringing back and helping to heal the wounded? What are some ways in which you personally can contribute to this effort?
7. If you have been hurt by people in the church, take some time to write down your feelings. If you are still feeling wounded, pray for God to prepare your heart to deal with the hurt and be healed of the pain.

—Part II—

THE WOUNDED LAMB

A Plan for Healing and Restoration

Chapter 6

LAMBENTATIONS

Encountering Hope in Our Good Shepherd

I'll recognize the sound of your voice.

PSALM 119:176

Because some of you are going to start reading this book here rather than at the beginning, I want to open with an important point from part 1. (And even if you have already read the first five chapters, it bears repeating.) When a shepherd discovers that one of his sheep is *cast,* that is, upside down and trapped, the shepherd does not abandon that fallen animal. He doesn't throw his hands up in exasperation and tell the sheep that she is on her own. Because he realizes the danger that a wandering and defenseless lamb faces, he drops everything and makes it his priority to right that sheep and carry her back to safety.

Even after all these years, I do not always apply that knowledge to my relationship with Christ, the Good Shepherd. I still imagine Jesus's being frustrated with my bumbling attempts at faith. Sometimes when my mistakes leave me cast in a brierpatch of sin, I think

He will surely give up on me. Yet that is not the message of Scripture. When I fall into trouble, He seeks me every time. He doesn't seek me only when I have met some criteria of correct behavior. Not just when I faithfully tithe or send money to a television evangelist. He seeks me *every time* I wander away. But an important corollary is that He won't force me to return against my will.

This section is written to the wounded lambs among us. Regardless of your experience with human shepherds, I want to begin with a clear picture of your true heavenly Shepherd, Jesus. The Bible portrays Jesus as the healer of His wounded sheep.

UNDER THE GOOD SHEPHERD'S WATCHFUL EYE

In order to understand this important point, we need to go back to the pasture. Jesus described Himself as the Good Shepherd in the gospel of John. The early Christians knew that a shepherd never would leave his flock; those sheep would be lost without his care.

In the following passage, the Lord explains that He is that type of shepherd to His church, which includes me and you.

> I am the Good Shepherd. The Good Shepherd puts
> the sheep before himself, sacrifices himself if neces-
> sary. A hired man is not a real shepherd. The sheep
> mean nothing to him. He sees a wolf come and runs
> for it, leaving the sheep to be ravaged and scattered
> by the wolf. He's only in it for the money. The sheep
> don't matter to him.
>
> I am the Good Shepherd. I know my own sheep
> and my own sheep know me. In the same way, the

Father knows me and I know the Father. I put the
sheep before myself, sacrificing myself if necessary.
You need to know that I have other sheep in addition
to those in this pen. I need to gather and bring them,
too. They'll also recognize my voice. Then it will be
one flock, one Shepherd. (John 10:11-16)

Jesus clearly noted the difference between the real shepherd and
the "hired man." Only the real shepherd cares enough to sacrifice his
own life to save the sheep. When I speak with wounded lambs, I learn
that they have often been victims of a hired-hand shepherd. They
have learned from his actions that they apparently meant nothing to
that shepherd. Experiencing great pain and heartbreak, they found
that the hired hand didn't protect the weak and injured lambs. And
all of us can probably cite examples of the hired-hand shepherd who
seems to be in it only for the money, power, or control he or she has
over a flock. All of these actions and attitudes grieve Christ, wound
the sheep, and damage the flock.

As I explained in part 1, Scripture warns us that this can happen.
When it does, Jesus advises us to turn our eyes to Him. He is the
Good Shepherd who understands the pain, betrayal, and anguish that
such selfish and sinful behavior causes. Listen for His voice. He is calling you.

When a shepherd calls his sheep, only those lambs that know that
particular shepherd will respond. Now, shepherds don't function like
the cowboys in the Old West movies. Imagine a cowboy riding out
among mixed herds of cattle from several different ranches. Picture
him tenderly calling the cows from the Bar None Ranch to come on
in fer feedin' time. I suspect the cattle would give him that same

befuddled look that your kids give you when you ask them to do work around the house. But if two flocks of sheep are intermingled, they can separate themselves and follow the voice of the shepherd they know. How cool is that?

What an incredible picture of how we can listen for the voice of our Good Shepherd. If we do, we will hear Him. While I am not one who claims to hear the audible voice of God on a regular basis, I can tell you that His overwhelming presence has sustained Joni and me through some pretty rough times.

Sheep who are secure in the presence of their shepherd seem to lack an awareness of the extent to which they are watched over. They go merrily on their woolly way, grazing happily without any acknowledgment that the shepherd has just dispatched a pack of wild dogs or steered them away from a dangerous ravine or bypassed unsafe water.

I picture myself (and you) like those comically clueless sheep. We have no idea that our Good Shepherd has steered us away from danger or gently led us to a safer place. Instead, as humans, we tend to focus on the times God didn't seem to do His job. We wonder, *How could God let this happen?* When our daughter Katie was born with a terminal birth defect, someone asked me, "Why did this have to happen to you?" Yet I have never been asked why Joni and I have three healthy and wonderful sons. No one has ever asked me why I have been blessed with good health for fifty years when others more godly than I struggle daily to breathe or never experience the bliss of a pain-free day. As the saying goes, "If you haven't all the things you want, be grateful for the things you don't have that you didn't want."

I think that most of us, when we read the passage from John about the Good Shepherd, tend to think Jesus was speaking only of the entire body of Christ. Allow me to personalize the words of Christ and see how that changes your perspective on His incredible provision in your life:

> I am the Good Shepherd. The Good Shepherd puts *you* before himself, sacrifices himself if necessary. A hired man is not a real shepherd. *You* mean nothing to him. He sees a wolf coming and runs for it, leaving *you* to be ravaged and scattered by the wolf. He's only in it for the money. *You* don't matter to him.
>
> I am the Good Shepherd. I know *you* and *you* know me. In the same way, the Father knows me and I know the Father. I put *you* before myself, sacrificing myself for *you* if necessary. (see John 10:11-16)

So let us begin a candid discussion of our woundedness with this important truth: We have a Lord who knows us by name, put us before Himself and died on the cross, and values us beyond measure. We are priceless to Him. That should be a message of incredible comfort to every wounded lamb.

KILLING OUR WOUNDED

Too often, however, unloving or unaware members of the flock preach a different message, one that compounds woundedness and fuels guilt instead of pointing struggling lambs to the healing grace of the Good Shepherd.

An uncomfortable scene from the movie *Forrest Gump* illustrates what can happen when believers insensitively address wounded lambs about their pain and loss. The dialogue is uncomfortable because every thinking believer has had to confront the issue of how a loving God can be truly involved in the world and yet allow terrible things to happen. Forrest saved his commanding officer, Lieutenant Dan, from death in Vietnam, but during the battle the man lost both legs. An embittered Lieutenant Dan has this exchange with the naive Gump:

Lt. Dan: Have you found Jesus yet, Gump?

Forrest: I didn't know I was supposed to be looking for him, sir.

Lt. Dan: That's all these cripples, down at the V.A., that's all they ever talk about. Jesus this and Jesus that. Have I found Jesus? They even had a priest come and talk to me. He said God is listening, but I have to help myself. Now, if I accept Jesus into my heart, I'll get to walk beside him in the kingdom of heaven. Did you hear what I said? Walk beside him in the kingdom of heaven. Well, kiss my crippled ***. God is listening. What a crock.

Forgive me if that dialogue offends you. But Lt. Dan was honest. And his is the kind of emotional response you might offer (or at least think) when you're wounded by life, by others, and especially by the church. It also contains misconceptions many of us have about God. Tragically, some of the misconceptions are a result of the things that Christians have communicated about the trials that life brings.

WHY DO BAD THINGS HAPPEN TO GOOD PEOPLE?

When Katie was born, some Christians told us she would be healed if we only "had enough faith." What a crippling accusation. Or how about Christians saying to a parent who has lost a child, "God needed another angel in heaven." So God capriciously picks off children for His own pleasure? I have also encountered Christians who blithely throw down that "all things work together for good" scripture without the context that qualifies and defines the promise.

Even though their intent is often to comfort, most of us would be far better off if our "comforters" said nothing rather than tried to explain or justify the tragedies of life. During Katie's brief stay on earth, Joni and I found the mere presence of sympathetic friends more comforting than anything else.

Tragedy has always been a part of our world. Even Jesus, when asked to explain why some Galilean followers had been murdered by Pilate, did not get specific. Was it sin in the lives of those poor victims that caused them to be killed? Jesus responded:

> Do you think those murdered Galileans were worse sin-
> ners than all other Galileans? Not at all. (Luke 13:2-3)

Jesus went on to comment about another fatal accident:

> And those eighteen in Jerusalem the other day, the
> ones crushed and killed when the Tower of Siloam
> collapsed and fell on them, do you think they were
> worse citizens than all other Jerusalemites? Not at all.
> (Luke 13:4-5)

Let's see now. Jesus wouldn't acknowledge any connection between sin and tragedy, but I have encountered many Christians who do. On another occasion, Jesus was asked whose sin was responsible for a man's blindness. His disciples asked:

> "Rabbi, who sinned: this man or his parents, causing him to be born blind?"
>
> Jesus said, "You're asking the wrong question. You're looking for someone to blame. There is no such cause-effect here. Look instead for what God can do." (John 9:2-3)

Again, if Jesus refused to assign blame or explain away tragedy, I am not about to try. When specifically asked the question, Jesus said there was no correlation between sin and death by murder, between sin and death by accident, or between sin and physical handicap.

Yes, I am aware that some sins and afflictions do have cause-and-effect connections. Taking drugs during pregnancy can lead to tragic results. And I know there are instances documented in Scripture where God caused affliction and even death because of disobedience. I also know that Paul wrote that certain sins can hasten death. It is common sense that drunk driving or heavy smoking, for example, might lead to an early demise.

My point is that when Jesus had the chance to make a direct connection between life's tragedies and our spiritual condition, He refused. Devastating events sometimes just happen. Why? "You're asking the wrong question," Jesus said. In truth, we will never have the answer this side of heaven. Instead, the healing message from Jesus is to "look instead for what God can do."

My heart goes out to every reader of this book who is a wounded lamb. Please realize you are not alone. We have in our midst millions of wounded, abandoned, and hurting lambs. Isn't that an odd comfort? I have talked to so many people who thought they were the only ones who have been the targets of spiritual drive-by shootings at their churches.

I know how much it hurts to be wounded by the flock. But I also pray that you will look to the Good Shepherd and see what God can do in you and for you during these difficult, pain-filled days. He cares about your hurt. He grieves when you grieve. And as we saw from the example of Job's friends in chapter 5, He is angry when you, one of His precious lambs, are injured by other sheep or shepherds. Without wanting to resort to spiritual saber-rattling, I pray that you will reach a point where you can believe that such bad flockmates will have their own day of reckoning. In the meantime, let God surprise you with what He can do in your life.

GUILT IS A SYMPTOM, NOT A DESTINATION

I also pray that you won't feel like a "bad Christian" if you respond to those who hurt you in a way that surprises or even embarrasses you. When we are hurt, our very natural tendency is to hurt back. But that natural tendency is also the reason we need to take our hurts to the Good Shepherd for healing. After you have been comforted in Christ, you can begin the process of forgiveness and reconciliation, which we will explore later.

When wounded lambs are feeling the pain of their life, it's easy for the Enemy to keep them in the throes of guilt. Resist this trap. Guilt is never a destination or even a resting place in our walk with

Christ. But I've noticed that wounded lambs have a hard time seeing the difference between *feeling guilty* and *being guilty*. Just as children might feel guilty when their parents divorce, injured sheep can feel guilty when a church situation explodes. They might believe it is somehow their fault, even if it isn't. When wounded lambs do own any blame for their situation, they usually already feel guilty about it. Even if they aren't to blame, Satan certainly loves to plant the idea in their minds that they're at fault for their own suffering.

Now guilt can be a positive emotion when it leads us to recognize and repent of our sin. But guilt should be merely a precursor to redemptive action, not a nagging reminder of personal failure. Philip Yancey wrote, "I now realize that Christians are the only persons who do not have to go through life feeling guilty. Guilt is only a symptom; we listen to it because it drives us toward the cure."[1]

That is definitely how God intended to use guilt in our lives. We have to first know we are sick if we are going to choose to be cured. And guilt can lead us to identify our sickness. Our next step is to go to the Good Shepherd for both the diagnosis from His Word and Spirit and a prescription of healing forgiveness and grace.

NOBODY KNOWS THE TROUBLES WE'LL FACE

I believe that one of the biggest mistakes we Christians have made in our zeal and desire to show Christianity as attractive is to minimize the cost of following Jesus. This walk with Jesus wasn't designed to be easy. Certainly "Jesus is the answer" to the questions pertaining to purpose in life, significance, and eternity. But the hackneyed catch phrase may suggest to some that our every problem will be replaced by unending serenity and joy. Jesus is not a money-back guarantee for perfect health, unlimited prosperity, and nonstop giddiness.

Jesus offered only one guarantee concerning trouble in our lives: He guaranteed we would experience it.

> Therefore do not worry about tomorrow, for tomorrow will worry about itself. Each day has enough trouble of its own. (Matthew 6:34, NIV)

Paul reinforced the very real cost of following Jesus:

> Anyone who wants to live all out for Christ is in for a lot of trouble; there's no getting around it. (2 Timothy 3:12)

Talking about the immature believer, Jesus said,

> But since he has no root, he lasts only a short time. When trouble or persecution comes because of the word, he quickly falls away. (Matthew 13:21, NIV)

Or, as the always-eloquent Mike Tyson said, "Everyone has a game plan until they get hit in the mouth." Many of us have not been prepared for the inevitable spiritual punch in the mouth that is coming from life, from the Enemy, and, sadly, sometimes from other Christians. We've been told, "Just give your troubles to Jesus." Our fellow sheep have neglected to point out that Jesus might allow those very troubles in order to shape our character and define our need for

Him. They also forget to mention that from those very troubles God will develop maturity and depth to our faith and that there is much value to be mined from those difficulties.

When facing a career-ending illness, NBA basketball star Alonzo Mourning said, "Adversity introduces a man to himself." When we face adversity, we discover whether our faith can stand up to the challenge. Does this faith work when the skies turn dark and the seas are rough?

Former UCLA football coach Pepper Rogers was a proponent of a certain complicated offense called the wishbone. When the team struggled through a difficult season, the alumni demanded that he change the system. "The wishbone," Rogers said, "is like Christianity. If you believe in it only till something goes wrong, you don't believe in it in the first place."[2] In many ways we, like that alumni group, question "the system" when trouble comes our way. When we do, only one of two truths applies: Either we don't actually believe the promises of Jesus, or we don't really know the promises He made to us in the Bible.

> I have told you these things, so that in me you
> may have peace. In this world you will have trouble.
> But take heart! I have overcome the world. (John
> 16:33, NIV)

What an incredible promise! To know that we can have peace, contentment, and a lack of fear in this world is a promise far greater than luxury cars, big homes, expensive clothes, and a trophy mate.

JESUS IS NOT THE ONE WHO LETS US DOWN

Instead of clinging to the peace of Christ, many of us go looking elsewhere to escape from our troubles. As I put down this writing, I happened upon an old televised sermon of the late preacher E. V. Hill. Brother Hill was preaching about the prosperity gospel. (Was it a coincidence that I happened to pause at that point and surf the channels? I think not.) E. V. attacked the topic in his own inimitable style. He rebuked some of his congregation for sending twenty dollars to a well-known television evangelist to receive a blessed handkerchief that would result in new cars and riches for them if they had enough faith. He noted that all were twenty dollars poorer, and all they had to show was *despair that Jesus had somehow let them down.* Then he hit them with the uncomfortable truth of the ministry of Christ: It was their greed and lack of knowledge of who Jesus is, not Jesus Himself, that let them down. "Jesus didn't come to give you no car," he thundered. "He didn't come to put a new suit on the man; He came to put a new man in the suit." It is rare indeed when I shout, "Amen!" to Christian television, but Pastor Hill got my hearty agreement. Hope he heard it in heaven.

I would lovingly suggest that most wounded lambs are too quick to blame God for the troubles that come their way. This is detrimental to their spiritual health. For example, I don't go to the doctor filled with anger because I am sick. The doctor is the one who can help me; he is not the cause of my sickness. I don't refuse to see the physician because I am furious that I am not well, but that is often our reaction to spiritual wounds. Instead of seeking the One who can heal, we prefer to be angry that He allowed the wound. Why should we expect the God who stayed His hand as Jesus endured the Cross to make our lives a veritable tiptoe through the tulips?

Do You Know Who I Think I Am?

Even those of us who know that God never promised a life free of pain and hurt seem to expect that our insider relationship with Him will make pain, suffering, and hurt pass over us. As illogical as it is, we often expect perks like this to be among the benefits of our relationship with God.

I see the mentality when I travel. Because I fly way too much, I have achieved elite status with two different airlines. This status often puts me in the company of other frequent flyers who have also achieved a special relationship with the airline. I regularly witness irate, rude, and often profane people demanding that they receive special treatment because of who they are. "Do you realize that I have flown three million miles on your stupid airline," they snort, "and you can't allow me to change my flight without a penalty?" I confess I have often had that same mentality: "I am special. Look. I carry a Titanium Platinum Snotty Elite Card. Forget everybody else on the plane and let me on."

Have you ever caught yourself thinking in church like that frustrated flyer? *I have taught Sunday school for ten years and always missed the preaching service to do that. No one else would make such a sacrifice!* Or, *I have tithed faithfully to this church even when my own finances were not so good, and Mr. Hotshot Doctor and Hoity-Toity Lawyer probably don't give much at all. So why are You sending this affliction on me, God? How about doing this to someone who is not doing as much as I am? Doesn't my status in the church mean anything to You?* It looks a bit unseemly in print, but we tend to think this way when bad things happen to us.

Our Good Shepherd Was Wounded Too

Here's more comfort worth clinging to: We have a Savior who understands our wounds. Of all the people who could have claimed elite status, surely the Son of God fit the bill. But He was mocked, spat upon, humiliated, beaten, and scorned. He was deserted by the very men He had poured every ounce of Himself into for three years. He was rejected by the people He came to minister to. He was crucified for telling the truth. When I compare my wounds to those of Jesus, I am quite sure that He can comprehend the depth of my hurts. He could have exacted revenge and annihilated those who wounded Him, yet Jesus chose not to violate His Father's will. In fact, He spoke these haunting words from the cross:

> Father, forgive them; they don't know what they're
> doing. (Luke 23:34)

We will have troubles. We will be wounded. Count on it. But Paul had a good word for the folks in Rome—and for us—when he wrote:

> Who shall separate us from the love of Christ? Shall
> trouble or hardship or persecution or famine or
> nakedness or danger or sword? (Romans 8:35, NIV)

Nothing can separate us from the powerful love of our Good Shepherd, and as Christians we must cling tightly to that promise.

Paul added that our "light and momentary troubles are achieving for us an eternal glory that far outweighs them all" (2 Corinthians 4:17, NIV). Certainly at times our troubles don't feel light, let alone momentary. But in the perspective of eternity and the glory that awaits us, they are bearable.

SOMEDAY...THE REST OF THE STORY

It's true: God can shape adversity in our lives into something good. We tend to forget that our lives are scripts in progress and that we don't know the ending. We don't know the plot twists along the way. We can't always see how each one is related to the next and how everything will eventually intersect. We are in the midst of a story that God sees from the prologue to the epilogue. Only when the end credits roll will we begin to see how the pieces all fit together.

The movie *Signs* suggests that nothing in life happens by accident. The script clearly communicates that God uses every adverse circumstance and tragic event in His overall mosaic. While the film contained some concepts I disagreed with, the illustration of how God sovereignly weaves events together was fascinating.

And He does know best. Think about things you've prayed for. So often what we hope for in life would not be a gift at all. Garth Brooks sang a song titled "Thank God for Unanswered Prayers." In the song, a person comes to understand that all the things he once begged God for would not have been as good as the life he had been given. I think, when we get to the end of our run, we will see that God demonstrated His love by graciously refusing to answer some of our selfish and shortsighted prayers.

When I review some of the things I fervently prayed for in the past, I am grateful that certain petitions were denied. Some I still wish God had granted, but I have learned to trust Him until I see the whole picture. For example, I know that certain moments I once considered some of the worst in my life were important experiences, and I am actually grateful for them. In many of those spiritual valleys, you could not have begun to convince me that God was molding me or that those experiences could ever be of value. I knew the scripture just as you likely do: "In all things God works for the good of those who love him" (Romans 8:28, NIV). I now realize that mere knowledge of that promise is not enough. It comes down to our foundational belief of who God is. Do we believe His Word? I mean *really* believe His Word? That He will actually cause even the worst event to somehow work for our good or someone else's? That requires faith in a God who is trustworthy. Do we know His attributes? Do we believe— really believe—His promises? If we do, then we must accept the troubles, "sure that every detail in our lives of love for God is worked into something good" (Romans 8:28).

I have developed a heart of compassion for those of you who are wounded. Why? Because God gave me the privilege of being wounded early in my life.

That last sentence sounds crazy. Calling a wounding "a privilege" is not something I could have done twenty, ten, or perhaps even five years ago. But I can see that my struggles as an overweight, geeky, and generally outcast adolescent molded my heart to empathize with those who are hurt and ostracized by their peers. The truth of Paul's message to the Corinthians now makes sense to me.

Praise be to the God and Father of our Lord Jesus Christ,
the Father of compassion and the God of all comfort,

who comforts us in all our troubles, so that we can comfort those in any trouble with the comfort we ourselves
have received from God. For just as the sufferings of
Christ flow over into our lives, so also through Christ
our comfort overflows. (2 Corinthians 1:3-5, NIV)

Had I been the coolest guy or the best athlete or the most hand-
some dude, I most likely would not have developed a sensitive spirit
to others. So God gave me the opportunity on all of those fronts to
become more sensitive. I did not enjoy that period of my life. I would
have given anything at that time to be one of the popular kids. I
would have gladly traded nearly anything to be the starting quarter-
back or the big man on campus.

With the benefit of hindsight, I tell you the truth when I say that
I am grateful for every refining difficulty and problem I have experienced. Such a dramatic change in attitude came over time, through
growth in my relationship with Jesus and my trust in the truth of His
promises. As G. K. Chesterton wryly noted, "Do not free a camel of
the burden of his hump; you may be freeing him from being a
camel." Had I been freed of the burden of my "hump" (that tough
teenage passage), I would not be who I am today.

Hope in a Healing Touch

A recent experience with our canine senior citizen, Charlie, gave me
a little hint of how our relationship with the Good Shepherd Jesus
might work. At the ripe old age of twelve, Charlie suffered a health
crisis. He developed a large benign tumor under his front leg that
made walking difficult. We took him in for what would be a serious

surgery, and the vet did a masterful job of removing the growth and taking care of Charlie. Afterward, we went to the animal hospital to pick up the old guy.

We sat in the waiting room as they went to get Charlie. He shuffled slowly out, and I was taken aback by his appearance. Charlie was trembling and frightened. He appeared to be in some pain. His head was down and his perpetual-motion tail was strangely still. He seemed confused and disoriented. Then I walked over to Charlie and simply touched him. Almost immediately he quit trembling and made a valiant attempt to wag his tail. We carefully got Charlie into the car and took him home to heal.

As I reflected on that scene, it struck me that the impact of my touch and mere presence with Charlie was a wonderful illustration of how Jesus comforts (or desires to comfort) His sheep. When I (his master) touched Charlie, he was comforted. His pain didn't disappear. He was still frightened. He was still a bit disoriented and unsure. Charlie's circumstances hadn't really changed at all. But he knew that his master was there, and that improved his outlook.

The touch of Jesus enables us to look to Him when we are frightened, in pain, disoriented, and confused. Jesus has promised that He will be with us in troubling times and that His presence will give us all the strength we need to make it through. Again the tough question arises: Do we truly believe Him?

The Good Shepherd Knows What Each Lamb Needs

Right after Jesus had finished His Sermon on the Mount, He came down from the mountain "with the cheers of the crowd still ringing in his ears" (Matthew 8:1). This description brings to mind a movie star arriving at a premiere. Get the setting here. Jesus had just delivered a powerful and culture-rattling message. Throngs of admirers followed Him down the mountain, and the people chattered excitedly about the amazing things He had just said.

Suddenly everything came to a stop as a leper appeared and fell on his knees before Jesus. I imagine no one in the crowd knew quite what to do. A leper was legally forbidden to interact with anyone, let alone with this remarkable new teacher. The tragic victims of this disfiguring and thought-to-be highly contagious disease were required to yell, "Unclean!" whenever another person came by. No one would even consider touching a leper. Should the crowd rebuke the diseased man? Should they summon the priests? What would Jesus do in the face of this outrageous violation of religious and social protocol?

I also imagine that the leper knew exactly what he was doing. Something about Jesus had touched his spirit and told him that this teacher was different. And this hurting and very abandoned lamb seized his chance to be healed from his woundedness. The leper spoke:

> Master, if you want to, you can heal my body.
> (Matthew 8:2)

The ravaged man could not bring himself to expect healing. But he had faith that Jesus had the power to heal his pain if He desired. It was a simple, childlike, and yet amazingly bold and courageous move. What the Good Shepherd Jesus did is a definitive example of His reaching out with grace for His wounded lambs.

> Jesus reached out and touched him. (verse 3)

For the first time in years, maybe decades, someone touched him. The gesture brings to mind the lyrics of a song written by Bill Gaither about Jesus that I used to sing in Sunday school. "He touched me, oh He touched me. And oh, the joy that floods my soul."

Can you imagine the joy the Good Shepherd's gesture gave the leper? Can you imagine the shocking impact it must have had on that already-unsettled crowd? Jesus didn't have to touch him. He could have merely spoken a word and healed the man. In the gospel of John, Jesus proved that He didn't even have to be in the same ZIP code to heal someone.

> When [the official] heard that Jesus had come from Judea to Galilee, he went and asked that he come down and heal his son, who was on the brink of death. Jesus put him off: "Unless you people are dazzled by a miracle, you refuse to believe."
>
> But the court official wouldn't be put off. "Come down! It's life or death for my son."
>
> Jesus simply replied, "Go home. Your son lives."
>
> The man believed the bare word Jesus spoke and headed home. On his way back, his servants intercepted him and announced, "Your son lives!"
>
> He asked them what time he began to get better. They said, "The fever broke yesterday afternoon at one o'clock." The father knew that that was the very moment Jesus had said, "Your son lives." (John 4:47-53)

But in the case of the leper, Jesus knew what this wounded lamb needed to be fully healed: The leper needed to be touched. The Lord answered the desperate man's plea, uttered in last-ditch desperation, "If you want to..." And Jesus "touched him, saying, 'I want to. Be clean.'" (Matthew 8:3)

"I want to. Be clean." That phrase can be a healing balm for the soul of a wounded lamb. If you feel untouchable, He is willing to reach out and embrace you. Even if you feel as if no one wants to heal you, Jesus wants to see you restored. And if you feel unclean, He wants you to feel His cleansing power.

Certainly the flock has a responsibility to seek you if you are wounded. I have spent most of this book so far reiterating that truth in as many ways as I know how, but some will not obey that biblical command. The undeniable good news, however, is that Jesus the Good Shepherd *is* seeking you. He *wants* to heal you, even if the actions (or inaction) of the shepherds and the flock suggest otherwise. You don't even need to say, "If you want to..." Know that He does.

The real question is, Do you want Him to heal you? We're about to test the truth of your answer. Are you ready to give up whatever is keeping you from accepting His healing touch?

— For Reflection and Discussion —

1. What is Jesus's response to you when you sin?
2. Read the description of the Good Shepherd on page 116. What are the differences between the hired hand and the Good Shepherd?
3. What do you think Jesus meant when He said His sheep will know His voice? Did He mean an audible voice? How do you hear His voice in your own life?

4. What is the significance of the examples that Jesus cited in Luke 13:1-5?

5. When has God used adversity in your life to grow your character or intimacy with Him? Write down one example.

6. Why do you think Christians are often so discouraged by their troubles?

7. Name one promise that Jesus made concerning trouble—other than the promise that you will surely have it! If you are going through a tough time, claim that promise by writing it down, praying about it, and reviewing it every day.

Chapter 7

YOUR BLEATING HEART (WILL TELL ON YOU)

Letting Go of Victimhood

As scarce as truth is, the supply is always greater than the demand.

JOSH BILLINGS

In this chapter I am going to focus on a thread of truth that I pray will be woven lovingly into a tapestry of humility and grace. I confess that writing this chapter filled me with more fear and trembling than any topic I have yet tackled (except politics). I pray that my tone reflects the spirit of the Hippocratic Oath—that I "do no harm." If I do not create an atmosphere of love, the truth of this chapter could do damage and that would break my heart. This may be the most important chapter in the book.

I hope this book will be read by many wounded lambs. Some of you have been abused by shepherds who should have restored you but instead chose to condemn you (or worse). Some of you have been neglected by churchgoers who should have cared enough to seek you out and return you to the flock. And I do not deny that many of us have been victims of the sinful, selfish, and hurtful acts of those in and around the church.

But we must also acknowledge (time to duck and cover) the real possibility that sometimes we choose to remain victims when we have the opportunity to move on. A wounded lamb cannot be healed while clinging to victimhood. One of my prayers and goals for this book is that we would honestly search our hearts and prayerfully evaluate if we have, in fact, made a decision to hang on to our woundedness.

It is an incredible waste of our spiritual potential to fixate on how events of the past could have or should have been different. Most of us who have been hurt could persuade any jury that the treatment we received from other Christians *should have been* different. We can make a solid case based on the wisdom and conviction of Scripture that things *would have been* different if Christians consistently applied Christ's words. It took me about forty-five years to figure out the following information that I am going to pass along to you (at no additional cost) for simply buying this book. Are you ready?

THINGS ARE NOT DIFFERENT.

No amount of time spent dwelling on how another sheep hurt us or should have done something different will change our present situation.

Imagine that you have been shot and rushed to the emergency

room. Would you spend all of your time worrying about who shot you? Or do you think your first concern might be to survive? I am pretty sure that my priority would be to seek help and healing. Who shot me would be the least of my worries at that point. After I heal, I can concern myself with the shooter and whether justice is done.

With physical hurts, we immediately seek help. But emotional and spiritual hurts seem to engender a response unlike any other wound. When we are "shot" by people in the church, we have a tendency to focus on the shooter, not the Healer. This is one of our Enemy's most effective distraction strategies—he knows that healing is available, and he does not want us to get it. The last place Satan wants us to visit is the emergency room of God's grace. As far as Christians are concerned, the act of healing allows us to leave justice in the hands of God, a holy and righteous judge, and takes us out of the process. That is exactly where we need to be.

Those of us who have been wounded could probably benefit from becoming more aware of Satan's desire to keep us firmly in the grip of victimhood. Playwright Eugene O'Neill wrote, "Man is born broke. He lives by mending. The grace of God is glue."[1] Satan would have us forget that being broken is an integral part of God's plan for our growth and that God does, in fact, mend us with His grace. The apostle Paul, who begged God to remove his affliction, or "thorn in the flesh," came to an important realization:

> And then he told me,
> "My grace is enough; it's all you need.
> My strength comes into its own in your weakness."
> Once I heard that, I was glad to let it happen. I

quit focusing on the handicap and began appreciating
the gift. It was a case of Christ's strength moving in
on my weakness. (2 Corinthians 12:9)

Paul "quit focusing on the handicap." This action is essential to
our recovery. Sadly, many of us stop acting when we are broken. This
point of resignation is heartbreakingly just short of the point where
we can receive God's healing.

RULES OF ENGAGEMENT

Why are the wounds suffered at church so devastating? Perhaps
because we don't expect the rules of street fighting to be present there.
But low blows like gossip, manipulation, backstabbing, and so on, do
find their way into the body of Christ.

I wrote most of this book while the United States was at war with
Iraq. A big topic during this time was the rules of engagement for the
military. Many nations believe there are certain rules about how to
fight a war that should never be violated. For example, a hospital
should never be used to shield troops and weapons. Strategic military
targets should not be located near churches or schools. Soldiers
should not hang out with civilians because of the potential danger to
innocents. During the Iraq war, our opponents did not share our
view of the rules of engagement. They were, in fact, willing to kill
many of their own citizens. Most of us found this highly disturbing.

Similarly, the real Enemy of Christians, Satan, does not share our
ideas for the rules of engagement. Jesus warned us of the inherent
dangers of being a lamb in this brutal world.

Stay alert. This is hazardous work I'm assigning you.
You're going to be like sheep running through a wolf
pack, so don't call attention to yourselves. Be as cunning as a snake, inoffensive as a dove. (Matthew 10:16)

We really are like sheep running through a wolf pack—both
inside and outside the church! I wish that were not the case, but we
don't have a screening system to investigate everyone who claims to
be a Christian. We let 'em all in, and some wolves find their way into
pews. (I spoke of this reality in part 1.)

Still, most Christians are simply not prepared to encounter the
tactics of the world inside the church. Everything seems dandy until
someone begins spreading the word that she saw you having a *glass of
wine* at a local restaurant. Or when a fellow leader takes you to task
for teaching from a book by an author (hopefully not me) who he
knows is apostate—and you would have known that too if you were
listening to the Holy Spirit! We are unprepared for this kind of unbib-
lical blindsiding.

You likely would not hurt a boxer if you took a swing at him in
the ring. He would be wary, fists up, ready to defend and respond.
You might hurt that same tough individual if you slugged him at the
dinner table when he was totally unprepared and defenseless, never
dreaming that an attack might happen in a supposedly safe place.
Some churchgoers view the church as a safe place (it should be) where
no sucker-punches could possibly be thrown. They believe they are
not at risk (they should not be) and can let their defenses down.

For many of us, church is a final attempt to find community, a
place to fit in. For others, the church is the last bastion of hope that

there is a place where they will not be hurt. Betrayal by a person in the church really does cause a hurt disproportionate to the size of the wound. The psalmist described the feeling in this passage:

> This isn't the neighborhood bully
>> mocking me—I could take that.
> This isn't a foreign devil spitting
>> invective—I could tune that out.
> It's you! We grew up together!
>> You! My best friend!
> Those long hours of leisure as we walked
>> arm in arm, God a third party to our conversa-
>> tion. (Psalm 55:12-14)

Can't you feel the pain of the writer? Haven't you been there at one time or another? *It's you! It's not Bob the Backstabber or Gertie the Gossip. I would have been ready for that. It's you! My best friend...or so I thought.* It does hurt disproportionately to the apparent size of the wound.

WHAT DO YOU MEAN I'M "DEFENSIVE"?!

I am going to be really honest with you about my normal reaction to those who wound me. First, I get defensive and angry. Next, I am overcome by the desire to get even. I am tempted to gossip, and my intent (if I am honest) is to dent my shooter's reputation. (Gossip is a very effective form of revenge. I can present it as "sharing my hurt with others" and still feel good about myself spiritually.) Mixed in all this is an occasional wish for bad things to befall the person (not real bad, just something uncomfortable). Yep, when someone hurts me, any response I have other than the decidedly unattractive list above is a direct result of Christ living through me.

Case in point: Most of the comments I received concerning *Bad Christians* were amazingly kind and full of grace. But when I was criticized, I had to guard against reacting as a victim. In the book, I made a candid call for Christians to be held responsible for the damage they do to others and to the church. The author of the following critique, who identified himself only as "a reader from Wayland, Ma.," felt that I had the problem all wrong. In fact, he was pretty sure that I was the problem. I will reproduce the comments along with a sampling of my typical reactions (in bracketed italics) when I shift into victim mode.

> Burchett (as is the case with virtually all his co-reli-
> gionists) *[What the heck is a co-religionist?]* misses the
> point: it is the belief system that fosters these abuses.
> A good example of the simplistic nature *["Simplistic?"*
> *You don't have to agree with me, but I'm not STUPID!]*
> of Burchett's arguments is to be found in his brief
> treatment of the concept of eternal damnation. He
> asserts that it isn't a concept that even requires justifi-
> cation; it is God's universe, we are his creations, and it
> is his prerogative to do with us as he will. *[Guilty,*
> *though I didn't say it nearly that offhandedly.]* It isn't
> Christians who are arrogant, it's the secular humanists
> and believers of other faith traditions who are actually
> the arrogant one, as they seek to question God's
> authority! Extremely childish. *[Childish??? How dare*

you call me childish! At least my words were not written from the safe haven of anonymity.]

Burchett mentions that he and his wife have (if I recall correctly) two sons *[No, moron, three.]*, at least one of whom is studying to be a minister. *[Wrong again, Sherlock. They are studying higher-education administration, sports management, and, at the point of this writing, veterinary medicine.]* I often wonder how conservative evangelicals and fundamentalists who have "unsaved" children envision the Day of Judgment (if they are even capable of that kind of projection). *[So you think we just believe these things to be mean and don't even think about the ramifications?]* Do they imagine that, as their child is being dragged off, kicking and screaming to an eternity in hell, that they will turn to God, and say, "Well, this is unpleasant, but as you are perfectly just, it isn't my place to question your will?" *[No, nothing could be further from how I view my God and His judgment.]* This is the implicit outcome of Burchett's thought processes *[Thanks for interpreting my thoughts for me.]*, but I'm sure that he doesn't see it. *[Bingo, I'm too stupid to really understand what I think.]* It is a belief system so appalling that it should be beneath the dignity of a human being to indulge in it *[Are you serious? And your hatred toward faith is not appalling?]*, and Burchett brings nothing new to the argument. *[Okay, you may have finally made a point.]* He is incapable of seeing that it is the belief system itself that is abusive. *[I have recently learned to dress myself, and I no longer need Velcro closures on my shoes.]* If you aren't an evangelical or fundamentalist, and have more than a few brain cells to rub together, don't waste your time. *[First of all, dingbat, the book was written for evangelicals. It is not an apologetic, and if you had a few brain cells to rub together, you would have realized that.]*

My goodness, that looks ugly in print. But that is my truthful response to being (in my mind) attacked. Poor little me!

Every year during the Easter season I am reminded of the agony that Jesus endured for me. The shame, the mockery, and the suffering of the Cross touch me deeply. Then I turn around and get all bent out of shape because some stranger called me stupid! After receiving this review, I dragged my wounded little heart to my lovely bride, Joni. I read the mean comments to her and waited for her to validate my anger. I waited for her to tell me I was smart and that the reader was stupid. I waited for her to tell me that I was not simplistic or childish. I waited for her to pat me on the back and tell me I was deep and mature and not bad looking for a middle-aged guy. And I waited. And waited.

She absorbed the whole critique and then responded, "You really need to pray for that person. He is obviously under a lot of spiritual conviction to be that angry." *What? That is not what I wanted to hear!* But it was what I needed to hear.

Whenever I inflate with pride, God uses Joni as His little hatpin. And I was deflated because my woundedness had not been validated.

MISERY LOVES COMPANY

Let me clarify that I am not questioning whether any of us has ever been victimized. Clearly, that's not uncommon. What I'm trying to do is challenge our typical response to that kind of pain. Anglican clergyman and novelist Charles Kingsley wrote, "If you wish to be miserable, you must think about yourself, about what you want, what you like, and what respect people ought to pay you. Then to you, nothing will be pure. You will spoil everything you touch; you will make sin and misery out of everything God sends you."[2]

I sometimes try to imagine how I would respond if I were a disinterested third party listening to my own whiny complaints. Would I agree with my case, or would I think the argument was self-centered and exaggerated? If I am honest with myself, the latter is usually the case.

There are indeed those people in the church who find their identity in woundedness. They find a hurt under every rock. That kind of thinking is tragic; it never leads to the peace, joy, and contentment that Jesus came to this planet to provide. Few in the church have taken victimhood to the subterranean level that Romanian Sandu Tudose achieved. When his wife ran off with another man, the seventy-four-year-old vowed to spend the rest of his life in a hole in the ground. His underground ode to bitterness is located in the town of Mera, Romania, and is outfitted with a bathroom, heater, and water tap. He has food delivered regularly and his garbage picked up once a week. While you may find his response childish, you certainly cannot say that he "doesn't know forgiveness from a hole in the ground." While we may laugh at the ridiculous excess of this man's response, we can achieve emotional and spiritual equivalence by burrowing into ourselves and never surfacing to live within a community of believers.

I pray that those mired in the muck of victimhood will be gently prodded by the Holy Spirit to get up and get out. I pray that those who are deeply wounded will find the courage to claim the supernatural resources of forgiveness available to all believers. (More on that in chapter 9.)

Popular Christian apologist and youth minister Josh McDowell made a worthwhile distinction between those who are broken and those who are just needy: "Broken people are much more receptive because they've realized how self-dependent and prideful they are. They are very open to the Holy Spirit's work in their lives. Needy people, though, may not know how to trust God with their struggles. They tend to suck the life out of whomever they come into contact with. Thus, we must help them learn how to talk to God about their problems instead of pouring them out on the first person who'll listen—which is often what happens."[3]

If you are broken, you have completed your prerequisite studies and are qualified to begin Recovery Class 101. And if you have a twinge from the Holy Spirit that you have become a little "needy," then we will explore some ways you can take that neediness to the Lord.

Holocaust survivor Corrie ten Boom once wrote that anything "too small to be turned into prayer is too small to be turned into a burden."[4] Prayer is a good first step for eliminating the neediness that victimhood engenders. I sometimes allow hurts to roil around in my mind until my emotions have gone on the rampage and the perpetrators become evil incarnate. But when I take this pain to the Lord and articulate the offenses to Him, they often don't seem quite as major.

Finding a Different Type of Company

I believe with all of my being that God will bring individuals, groups, or even a church into our lives to help meet our needs and bring about healing. But the reality is that we are at least partially responsible to make that happen.

As hard as it is when you're wounded, an important step toward giving up victimhood is to take time and invest yourself in the lives of a small group of people in the church. Not surprisingly, the best experiences that Joni and I have had in a church body coincided with our involvement in a dynamic small group. It takes work and time, but these relationships are worth the effort. Joni and I know there is a group of ten that will be there if we need them. We have no doubt. But that didn't happen by just waltzing through the church door on Sunday mornings. We have invested in their lives, and they in ours.

Without that kind of support from the flock, I think we are more likely to blame God for the failure of His people or, for that matter, for our own failure. I am guilty of evaluating God just as I evaluate friends and neighbors. I think writer Stacey Padrick got it correct when she wrote, "We call people good if they do what we want and make us happy. We apply the same criteria to God."[5] As I mentioned in chapter 6, to blame God for our wounds from others effectively leaves us marooned forever on Victimhood Island and brings our spiritual healing to a grinding halt.

Some churchgoers expect members of the flock to always be at their side when they experience a rough time. And that should be true. But what often happens is they get involved in a church filled with people like you and me who have our own problems. Oh, we care, but probably not enough to jeopardize the alignment of our own universe.

A more vexing problem is that some people in the church wound others freely, wholly convinced that they are following the teachings of Jesus. I would encourage you to examine their actions through the lens of God's Word. Perhaps part of your healing process will require finding a flock that properly balances doctrine and grace. The decision to leave a church is no small matter, but a church that will not facilitate your restoration and healing might require a change of flocks. A church that is abusive is not a place where any sheep should be, let alone a wounded lamb. And any shepherd who does not preach the gospel of Jesus Christ, the gospel of grace, should prompt you to seek a new flock. I would encourage you to review the checklist that I included in chapter 2 of *Bad Christians* to help evaluate whether the time has come for you to seek a new pasture. The grass isn't always greener elsewhere, but in some cases it may be more nourishing.

I must leave this topic with a word of caution. Please pray, be still, and listen—then, if you must, leave with grace and dignity. Burn no bridges and wound no sheep (or shepherds) as you exit.

No More Obstacles

In the gospel of John we see an example of how Christ asked a seeker to make a decision to leave his woundedness behind, knowing that he could never again fall back on that as his identity.

> Soon another Feast came around and Jesus was back
> in Jerusalem. Near the Sheep Gate in Jerusalem there

was a pool, in Hebrew called *Bethesda,* with five alcoves. Hundreds of sick people—blind, crippled, paralyzed—were in these alcoves. One man had been an invalid there for thirty-eight years. When Jesus saw him stretched out by the pool and knew how long he had been there, he said, "Do you want to get well?"

The sick man said, "Sir, when the water is stirred, I don't have anybody to put me in the pool. By the time I get there, somebody else is already in."

Jesus said, "Get up, take your bedroll, start walking." The man was healed on the spot. He picked up his bedroll and walked off. (John 5:1-9)

First, Jesus asked the invalid if he wanted to get well. What an amazing demonstration that God will not force Himself on anyone, no matter how obvious the need, if we don't make a decision to receive His healing. This man had apparently embraced victimhood for thirty-eight long years. So when Jesus asked him the question, the man launched into victim-speak instead of answering:

> Sir, when the water is stirred, I don't have anybody to put me in the pool. By the time I get there, somebody else is already in.

That did not answer Jesus's question. Still, Jesus showed grace mixed with a command to do something. "Get up," He said to the man. Jesus knew full well how much faith it would take to even attempt that seemingly simple task. When the man chose by faith to get up and leave his victimhood behind after nearly four decades, he was healed.

Father Alfred D'Souza wrote: "For a long time it had seemed to me that life was about to begin—real life. But there was always some obstacle in the way, something to be gotten through first, some unfinished business, time still to be served, a debt to be paid. Then life would begin. At last it dawned on me that these obstacles were my life."[6] I have come to that same realization regarding the church. These flawed people, these perceived obstacles to my joy, are the community that Jesus ordained for me. They are my fellowship life. Waiting for them to meet my needs will leave me frustrated till I depart this planet.

Is that a pessimistic view? I don't think so. I am also one of those flawed people, and those around me have to rely on the grace of Jesus to deal with me. The amount of energy invested in choosing bitterness or choosing healing is probably about the same. But the end results are diametrically different. One choice leaves me paralyzed in the past. The other choice gives hope for the future.

In the Christian walk, hurts are inevitable. Feeling like a victim and deciding to stay there really is optional.

CUT IT DOWN AND FORGET IT

If we choose to nurse our victimhood rather than treat our wounds, they can become spiritually life threatening. In the next two chapters, I'll take you through a few more steps toward healing. But if you have hit the spiritual wall of victimhood, my prayer is that you will decide this day to move past it.

A story is told about a visit the great General Robert E. Lee paid to a Kentucky home, where a bitter and angry woman pointed to what was left of a magnificent tree in front of her house. She was still upset that Union artillery fire had ruined the shape and beauty of the tree. She wanted General Lee to share her anger. She wanted the great leader to condemn the Yankees and sympathize with her. Lee paused and quietly said, "Cut it down, my dear Madam, and forget it."[7] Lee knew that the ravaged tree would only be a constant reminder of her victimhood. He wisely suggested that the reminder be cut out of her life so she could get on with her life. That tree would never be the same, and her bitterness would not change that fact.

I, too, have often chosen to turn scarred remnants in my own heart and mind into monuments that perpetually remind and upset me all over again. For many of us it is time to obey the words of Robert E. Lee: Let's cut it down, my dear brothers and sisters, and forget it.

— For Reflection and Discussion —

1. Why do people in the church have such a deep emotional reaction to wounds caused by or in the church?
2. Read 2 Corinthians 12:9. What change in Paul's attitude helped him to accept his handicap?
3. What was Jesus trying to tell us in Matthew 10:16? What are some ways in which you can follow His admonition to be "cunning as a snake, inoffensive as a dove"?
4. Describe the difference between a person who is broken and one who is needy. Are you broken or needy? Explain.
5. Why do you think Jesus asked the invalid in John 5 whether he wanted to be healed?

6. Are you holding on to something damaged or scarred in your life because you are angry about it? Name this thing. Ask Jesus to change your heart so you can, with His help, "cut it down and forget it."

Chapter 8

YOU HAVEN'T GOT TIME FOR THE PAIN

Choosing to Be Healed

You can outdistance that which is running after you, but not what is running inside you.

Rwandan Proverb

Aspen mountaineer Aron Ralston, twenty-seven, recently had to make a very desperate choice. An avid outdoorsman, he was rock climbing when a boulder, estimated to weigh at least eight hundred pounds, trapped his right arm. After a few days with no food or water, he had to make a horrible choice. Ralston determined that he had to amputate his arm in order to save himself. If he chose to wait for someone else to respond to his injury, he would most likely die. (An interesting sidebar is that no one was aware of how desperate his situation had become. He was often gone for long periods of time, so no one really panicked about his absence. I would suggest that sometimes our spiritual condition is like that. Others may have no idea how much we are hurt, how desperate the situation, and how trapped we feel because we have withdrawn. Some wounded lambs may be at a life-or-death spiritual point with no help in sight simply because they have not informed their brothers and sisters in Christ that they are trapped and desperate.)

Aron Ralston made the obviously excruciating decision to amputate his arm to save his life. I can guarantee you that he didn't feel like doing that. But he accomplished his grim task and survived.

You Can't Have One Without the Other

Our spiritual decisions to let go of victimhood and choose healing may not make headline news, but they just might save our lives. Choosing to let go of victimhood goes hand in hand with choosing to be healed. It is our choice to seek healing.

It took me a long time to learn that lesson, and occasionally I must go through remedial training. I do want to give up my woundedness and corresponding anger. Ask my wife. My anger toward someone who wounded me (or my family) used to have the shelf life of plutonium. I would have willingly sported a bumper sticker that said, "You can have my grudges when you pry them out of my cold dead fingers."

And I admit a certain comfort comes with holding anger close. It keeps us from having to face the painful truth of our personal responsibility to forgive and to seek or give healing. Theologian Frederick Buechner wrote, "Of the Seven Deadly Sins, anger is possibly the most fun. To lick your wounds, to smack your lips over grievances long past, to roll over your tongue the prospect of bitter confrontations still to come, to savor to the last toothsome morsel both the pain you are given and the pain you are giving back—in many ways it is a feast fit for a king. The chief drawback is that what you are wolfing down is yourself. The skeleton at the feast is you."[1] A graphic word picture—and deadly accurate.

What if we held on to anger, woundedness, and revenge in regard to life's physical hurts? I tried to imagine such a response to a physical wound. I love to ski, although I am not very skilled. While making a routine run down a fairly easy slope at Colorado's Copper Mountain, I was cut off by another skier who caused me to fall awkwardly. (That is a redundancy—I usually fall awkwardly.) Anyway, the fall dislocated my shoulder. It popped back into the socket, but I was still in a lot of pain.

If I had chosen to deal with this woundedness in the same way I react to a spiritual wound, I would have reveled in victimhood. I would have spent all my time dwelling on the stupidity of the person who cut me off. What a thoughtless person! I probably would have been filled with anger and seethed: Not only did she cause me to fall, but she skied on down the hill with no regard for my injury. I would have fixated on the fact that the skier made no attempt to apologize or stop to ask forgiveness for her stupid skiing! This jerk made no offer to aid in my medical care. She didn't even show a modicum of concern. I would have gone out of my way to tell others how I was wounded by this mountain moron. I would make sure I told everyone how this resort, which allowed selfish skiers like her on their slopes, was no longer a place where I felt welcome. I would spend every waking moment reliving the fall and remembering how that evil, conniving person deliberately sought an angle that gave me no option but to fall and endure a grievous injury.

If I actually dealt with my ski injury like that *and expected my shoulder to heal,* you would think I was an immature baby. Note as well how the emotions intensified as I let my victimhood fester.

Many wounds inflicted by people in the church are devastating in scope. But we should first examine the extent of the wounds to see if we might be making the injury worse than it really is by not giving it the right kind of attention. When I was a child, I stepped on a nail. The wound wasn't that bad, but my parents realized that I needed a tetanus shot to keep it from developing into something serious. If we are honest with ourselves, many of our spiritual wounds are really not that bad. But we need to take whatever steps we can to keep them from escalating into something worse.

So what actually happened on the ski slope that day? I was momentarily ticked at the person who cut me off, but I realized she was an inexperienced skier who meant me no harm and was far more concerned about her own survival than about hurting me. After a few moments I no longer thought about that skier. I let her go so I could concentrate on healing and getting rid of the pain. I sought out a clinic, got some x-rays and a painkiller, and wore a sling for a few days. My new focus was to make the pain go away, restore the use of my shoulder, and be healed from my injury.

What He Will Do for You

In the book of Mark, I see a fascinating example of how Jesus challenges us to choose healing:

> As Jesus was leaving town, trailed by his disciples and
> a parade of people, a blind beggar by the name of

Bartimaeus, son of Timaeus, was sitting alongside
the road. When he heard that Jesus the Nazarene was
passing by, he began to cry out, "Son of David, Jesus!
Mercy, have mercy on me!" Many tried to hush him
up, but he yelled all the louder, "Son of David!
Mercy, have mercy on me!"

Jesus stopped in his tracks. "Call him over."

They called him. "It's your lucky day! Get up!
He's calling you to come!" Throwing off his coat,
he was on his feet at once and came to Jesus.

Jesus said, "What can I do for you?" (10:46-51)

What a surprising question: *What can I do for you?* The crowd
knew what the man wanted. Jesus certainly knew what the man
wanted. But He also knew something else. What would having his
sight restored mean to a man who had been blind all his life? It would
mean he would no longer be able to live the life of a victim. No longer
would anyone feel sorry for him. No longer would his family provide
food for him because he could not work. His identity would no
longer be a tragic disability. He would now be a regular guy. The man
would now be responsible for himself, and Jesus knew what a big
change that would mean. Did he truly want to give up victimhood in
exchange for healing?

I like to consider what is not said as much as what is said. So here
goes. If I had suffered like the blind beggar, I might have a long list of
questions and wishes. But this man did not ask why he had to suffer
all those years without sight, never seeing a sunset, a spring flower, or
a human face. The blind man did not ask Jesus to punish those who

mocked him. He did not ask Jesus to exact revenge on every rich man who had callously passed by him with a condescending sniff or snide comment. There is no report that he chose any of those paths. His response was simple:

The blind man said, "Rabbi, I want to see." (verse 51)

Sometimes when I pray, I imagine Jesus asking me that question: "What can I do for you?" I wonder if we ever hear that quiet question from Jesus when we are shouting out in prayer (or gossip) about some jerk who wounded us or some church attendee who hurt us. We yell all the louder, just like the blind man. And that still, quiet voice asks, "What can I do for you?" It is an important question. Jesus knows that when I am wounded I often desire revenge or swift justice, but what I really need is healing. Only when I say, "Rabbi, I want to see (how to forgive)" or "I want to see (how I can love)" can I begin to be healed of my spiritual blindness.

Spiritual blindness can be more devastating than physical blindness. When we suffer spiritual blindness, we can see the beauty of flowers but not the beauty of forgiveness. When we are between the choices of victimhood or healing, we can find unexpected comfort and peace in simply being quiet and telling Jesus that we want to see through His eyes. Perhaps we should tell Him that we want to see what forgiveness looks like—how it blooms in the fertile soil of grace.

"On your way," said Jesus. "Your faith has saved and healed you."

In that very instant he recovered his sight and followed Jesus down the road. (verse 52)

Jesus asked the man what he wanted. As with the crippled man at Bethesda, He did not force Himself on this man, though his need was obvious. God's infinite resources are available to His sheep, but He has given us the freedom to choose.

BEHOLD THE POWER OF CHOICE

There's one thing we must remember about God's plan. Yes, God could intervene, but He chose to bless us with free will. Bless us? I think so. Would a forced obedience result in the kind of relationship you desire? I treasure my wife's love because she could *choose not to* love me, yet she *chooses to* love me. I think God feels a similar emotion when we choose to love Him. C. S. Lewis wrote about the mystery of free will:

> God created things that had free will. That means
> creatures which can go either wrong or right. Some
> people think they can imagine a creature which has
> free will but had no possibility of going wrong; I can-
> not. If a thing is free to be good it is also free to be
> bad. And free will is what made evil possible.[2]

Why, then, did God give them free will? Because free will, though it makes evil possible, is also the only thing that makes possible any love or goodness or joy worth having.

I have always been intrigued by why we human beings make certain choices. When confronted with the same options, why do some of us choose joy while others choose anger and bitterness? Is it a matter of knowledge? If we were better educated, would we make better choices? Or is choosing the better path simply an act of the will?

I think some of us make choices based only on what is easy, quick, and convenient. I have read countless books that I hoped would enable me to do something difficult with minimal effort and commitment. We prefer the easy diet or the easy fitness program. We prefer the instant fix.

But when we are wounded physically, the healing process sometimes involves a lengthy and painful physical therapy regime. In my world I see injured athletes going through the agony of rehabilitation after devastating injuries. What keeps them going through that painful process? At a minimum, the hope and belief that they will again be able to perform at their best without debilitating pain.

When we Christians need healing for our spiritual wounds, Jesus provides what is necessary. But we must accept the very real prospect that true healing may entail a long and painful process. We can be motivated by the hope and belief that we can rejoin the flock without debilitating pain.

Understand that while anger is a legitimate part of the healing process, we cannot afford to get stuck there. So try to step back and view the entire landscape of your walk with Jesus—what He has done for you and what He has promised for you when you hang in there. I pray that you will choose the path of healing. That is the goal. In fact, that is a requirement for followers of Christ.

Jesus's Choice

Jesus Himself had to face the agony of choosing what He should do in response to the hurtful betrayal by the "religious" leaders. I cannot begin to fathom the choice that Jesus had to make. While you and I are often powerless, Jesus had the power necessary to change the situation. He knew how indescribably agonizing the betrayal, trial, and crucifixion would be. What was Jesus's response to these trials in His earthly experience? He went off by Himself and found a quiet place to pray. Matthew tells us:

> He fell on his face, praying, "My Father, if there is
> any way, get me out of this. But please, not what
> I want. You, what do you want?" (26:39)

Wounded Christians who really understand the compassion of our Lord will pray honestly. We will express our hurts, desires, perceived needs, and even our unsavory feelings. But ultimately, if we really understand the sacrifice Christ made for us, we will choose to finish with the words of Jesus: "But please, not what I want. You, what do you want?"

I suspect that part of our reticence to choose healing stems from our fear. Fear of the unknown. Perhaps a fear of what God will find or require of us when our brokenness is exposed in His presence. Most of us have a real desire for privacy. One of our buzzwords in Christian circles is that we must be transparent. I find that I tend to be, at best, opaque. One of Satan's strategies is to make us believe that the cost of opening every area of our lives for Jesus to inspect will be far greater than the pain of living in secrecy. That (no surprise) is a lie.

His Wounds Become Your Healing

I imagine few people knew Peter as Jesus did. Peter's story is one of painful failure. His heartbreaking denial of Jesus is recorded in the gospel of Matthew:

All this time, Peter was sitting out in the courtyard. One servant girl came up to him and said, "You were with Jesus the Galilean."

In front of everybody there, he denied it. "I don't know what you're talking about."

As he moved over toward the gate, someone else said to the people there, "This man was with Jesus the Nazarene."

Again he denied it, salting his denial with an oath: "I swear, I never laid eyes on the man."

Shortly after that, some bystanders approached Peter. "You've got to be one of them. Your accent gives you away."

Then he got really nervous and swore. "I don't know the man!"

Just then a rooster crowed. Peter remembered what Jesus had said: "Before the rooster crows, you will deny me three times." He went out and cried and cried and cried. (26:69-75)

Peter was inconsolable after Jesus was arrested and crucified. Can you imagine a more devastating experience? Peter had walked with Jesus every day for three years. He had eaten, fished, laughed, and prayed with Him. Peter had participated in face-to-face discussions with Jesus that we would give almost anything to experience. Yet he failed Jesus miserably. Did that betrayal result in the Good Shepherd's leaving Peter and moving on? No. Jesus made a point of seeking out Peter after His resurrection. He accepted Peter, forgave him, and restored him.

Later, this once-devastated man wrote the words of 1 Peter 2:20-25 to wounded lambs. This passage was written to people who were slaves, caught in the oppressive economic system of the day. They had much in their lives to be bitter and angry about. But Peter assigned value and hope to their lives. The "Peter Principles" I've drawn from his words are lessons he learned at the feet of a Good Shepherd who intentionally sought out a sheep who had betrayed Him and then granted him restoration. Take a moment to meditate on Peter's message:

Peter Principle 1: God Sees Our Hearts and Actions

> There's no particular virtue in accepting punish-
> ment that you well deserve. But if you're treated
> badly for good behavior and continue in spite of
> it to be a good servant, that is what counts with
> God. (1 Peter 2:20)

If you are a wounded lamb who was injured without cause, your choice to forgive and be healed "counts with God." It is duly noted when you maintain a godly spirit when unfairly hurt.

Peter Principle 2: The Miracle of Jesus's Becoming Human Is That He Truly Understands Our Plight

> This is the kind of life you've been invited into,
> the kind of life Christ lived. He suffered everything
> that came his way so you would know that it could
> be done, and also know how to do it, step-by-step.
> (1 Peter 2:21)

So much of the hurt in this world can be traced to our inability to actually relate to other people because we cannot feel what they feel. I know I cannot fully understand the racism that African Americans feel because I have not been in their skin. Jesus has been in our skin. He went through all that we suffer to show us it can be done. But, more amazingly, He endured the suffering so that each of us has an empathic Good Shepherd to go to for guidance and strength.

Peter Principle 3: You May Be Attacked for No Cause

> He never did one thing wrong,
>> Not once said anything amiss.
>> They called him every name in the book and he
> said nothing back. He suffered in silence, content to
> let God set things right. (1 Peter 2:22-23)

But I must caution you to prayerfully see if a gentle examination by the Holy Spirit reveals anything you might need to repent of and repair before God and the flock. God will set things right in the final analysis. We have the responsibility to set our soul right before Him.

Peter Principle 4: His Redemptive Act Enables Our Healing

> He used his servant body to carry our sins to the
> Cross so we could be rid of sin, free to live the right
> way. His wounds became your healing. (1 Peter 2:24)

If anyone understood this principle, it was the once prideful Peter. He was a man who collapsed in tears after failing his Lord in the very way he swore he never would. But because Christ has experienced the wounds and felt the emotional pain that all of us feel, we are enabled to relate to God on a new level. Nothing in my experience is more healing or helpful than talking to someone who truly understands what I am going through. That is why support groups are so valuable. When Joni and I talk with parents who have had babies with terminal birth defects, we share an understanding, an emotional bond, and a freedom to safely express our feelings. That is what we have in Jesus. If I could communicate one truth to wounded lambs about Jesus, it would simply be this: He gets it. He understands. Because He was there. That is so hard for us as frail human beings to understand. But that is the miracle of God becoming man in Jesus.

> You were lost sheep with no idea who you were or
> where you were going. Now you're named and kept for
> good by the Shepherd of your souls. (1 Peter 2:25)

What a wonderful promise! The Good Shepherd knows us by name. We have everything we need to be healed and restored and "kept for good." Jesus understands our pain and shows us the path to healing.

But to be fully healed (why is there always a "but"?), we are asked to implement what I consider the toughest task of faith. It is called forgiveness. Part of choosing to be healed is releasing our offenders from retribution. In the Old Testament, we see how Joseph was betrayed by his own jealous brothers. Later he had the perfect opportunity to wreak revenge on their sorry heads. It was the kind of opportunity that most of us salivate over in our little fantasy visualizations about how we are going to exact payback. (I am currently undefeated in those imaginary battles!) Joseph had a real opportunity to get revenge when God delivered his conniving brothers right into his hands. All those years of torment and anger and hurt could now be deliciously vindicated. But Joseph made a choice.

Joseph chose to forgive them with the memorable statement, "You planned evil against me but God used those same plans for my good" (Genesis 50:20). I get chills when I read those words. How many times have I dreamed of getting the perfect opportunity to destroy someone verbally? Or I have wished that those who wounded me would someday find themselves desperately needing me, and I picture myself relishing the groveling apologies.

But not Joseph. He chose to honor God by forgiving his brothers when they did not deserve that act of compassion. That same supernatural power that enabled Joseph to offer grace to his brothers is available to you and me.

But how do we even begin to forgive those who often seem unforgivable? Take a deep breath, fasten your seatbelt, and turn to the next chapter. This ride may get a little bumpy.

— For Reflection and Discussion —

1. Reread Frederick Buechner's quote on pages 158-9. Do you ever find comfort in anger? Explain.

2. Why do we tend to treat spiritual wounds differently than we do physical wounds?

3. Read the story about the blind man in Mark 10:46-52. Compare Jesus's response to this man with His response to the leper He encountered in Matthew 8:1-4. Why did Jesus seem to make them choose healing before they were healed?

4. What did Jesus do to prepare Himself for the trial He would endure on the cross? In what ways could you adapt His attitude to your own sufferings?

5. If you are wounded, have you decided whether you want to be healed? If you do, take that choice to the Lord in prayer and tell Him you want to see healing. If something is hindering your prayers, ask God to help you identify the obstacle and remove it so that you can be healed.

Chapter 9

FORGIVENESS IS NOT OPTIONAL

Finding Supernatural Freedom

Nothing is impossible for the person who doesn't have to do it.

ANONYMOUS

Forgiveness may be the most unnatural thing that the Lord asks us to do. Forgiveness flies in the face of our inborn sense of justice. A man once commented to preacher John Wesley, "I never forgive." Wesley responded, "Then, sir, I hope that you never sin."[1]

A TROUBLING COMMAND

Literary great Mark Twain and I share at least one common sentiment. "Most people are bothered by those passages of Scripture they do not understand," he wrote, "but the passages that bother me are those I do understand."[2] Here are some passages that I completely understand and that have bothered me for years:

> In prayer there is a connection between what God
> does and what you do. You can't get forgiveness from
> God, for instance, without also forgiving others.
> (Matthew 6:14)

Could this be the reason why so many of us hit a spiritual plateau and just stay there? In our prayers we often seek special exemption for our situation: *Lord, You know how bad the people I have to deal with are, and I know that as a loving God You will cut me a little slack.* Actually, God's love is revealed in that He does not cut us any slack.

> And when you assume the posture of prayer, remember that it's not all asking. If you have anything against someone, forgive—only then will your heavenly Father be inclined to also wipe your slate clean of sins. (Mark 11:25)

"Only then," Jesus? You must understand how impossible it is for me to forgive that offense! Well, yes, He does understand perfectly how impossible it is to follow that command under our own strength, which is one more reason why following the teachings of Christ should cause us to give up on self and depend on Him.

> Be alert. If you see your friend going wrong, correct
> him. If he responds, forgive him. Even if it's personal
> against you and repeated seven times through the
> day, and seven times he says, "I'm sorry, I won't do
> it again," forgive him. (Luke 17:3-4)

Really now. Maybe I could manage once or twice, but doesn't continually forgiving make me a fool? Did You maybe misspeak there a little bit? Isn't it interesting how we will subconsciously wrestle with God about what He really meant? The text seems pretty clear in all of the translations. There are no exceptions.

> Be even-tempered, content with second place, quick
> to forgive an offense. Forgive as quickly and com-
> pletely as the Master forgave you. (Colossians 3:13)

The "as quickly" part is hard enough to obey. The "as completely" clause is nigh to impossible. And it can be almost as hard to accept second place as it is to be quick to forgive. That is another downside of being an American Christian. We are not rewarded in this society for being content with second place. I am very competitive. I love to win. But the desire to be first can be destructive. Jesus told us the "first shall be last," making the point that harboring a spiritual attitude of superiority had its own consequences. Your success in nailing down the committee leadership position or in the politicking to teach the Bible study will likely be your only reward. Don't be surprised when the one who humbly deferred to you will be rewarded in the heavenly bonus program.

Do you see a pattern in this sampling of verses on forgiveness? Do you see any way around the obvious command to forgive? Neither do I. And that causes me a bit of concern. Just like the average Christian, I want all the benefits of forgiveness without that annoying requirement that I actually have to forgive others. But the Bible is very clear about my responsibility to forgive. Forgiveness is a constant and, quite frankly, irritating theme of the New Testament. There do not appear to be any loopholes in these verses. I don't think we have a superspecies of unforgivable sins that have mutated since the days of Jesus that require a special dispensation. And I would imagine that Enoch at the tent-making shop was just as big a jerk as Bob in accounting. Bottom line: We are commanded to forgive as we have been forgiven. Straight up. No excuses.

A SUPERNATURAL ACT

Forgiveness may well be the missing ingredient for true revival in the church. Clearly our lack of forgiveness is a major impediment to personal and corporate growth. I believe that we attract people to Christ when we behave in a way that is supernatural. I'm not talking about performing miraculous healings or speaking in tongues. I'm talking about the supernatural behaviors radio host Steve Brown referred to: "We can claim to have supernatural love, but it's only supernatural when one would expect hatred instead. We can claim to be forgiving, but forgiveness is supernatural only when there is no earthly reason for one to be forgiving. Compassion is supernatural when the smart thing to do is look out for number one. Joy is supernatural when circumstances don't warrant it."[3]

What would be the result in our world if we demonstrated these supernatural aspects of Christ living through us? I suspect the unchurched would be clamoring to "get what we got." Forgiveness may be the singular act that convinces an unbelieving world that Christians really can be different. (Good different, not weird different.)

Suffering excruciating pain and indignity on the cross, Jesus gave an incredible demonstration of what supernatural forgiveness looks like:

> Jesus prayed, "Father, forgive them; they don't know
> what they're doing." Dividing up his clothes, they
> threw dice for them. (Luke 23:34)

Can you imagine a situation in which you would be less likely to want to forgive? Adding insult to injury, those around the cross mocked His amazing grace by gambling away His meager worldly possessions. Yet Jesus prayed for His Father to forgive them.

You may remember Reginald Denny. Following the Los Angeles trial verdicts in the emotionally charged Rodney King case, Denny was pulled from his truck at an intersection and beaten by an angry mob. Later Denny met his attackers, shook hands, and forgave them.

What was one media outlet's take on that act of grace? "It is said that Mr. Denny is suffering from brain damage." Forgiveness of such a monumental offense is hardly the normal human response. If that is brain damage, then may we all be afflicted just like Reginald Denny. Because Denny realized a fundamental truth outlined clearly in Scripture: Forgiveness is necessary to our spiritual and emotional healing.

ONE GOOD REASON

I was amused but heartened to see scientific research validating the emotional value of forgiveness. An article in *USA Today* tantalizingly titled "Psychologists Now Know What Makes People Happy," reported the findings of University of Michigan professor Christopher Peterson. (For this Ohio State Buckeye fan to agree with a Michigan prof shows the potential of grace in our lives.) Peterson stated that forgiveness is the behavior most strongly linked to happiness. Regular readers of the New Testament will not be surprised. The professor correctly noted, "It's the queen of all virtues and probably the hardest to come by."[4]

In this parable about a man forgiven a huge debt, Jesus revealed a secret about the reason to forgive:

> The kingdom of God is like a king who decided to
> square accounts with his servants. As he got under
> way, one servant was brought before him who had
> run up a debt of a hundred thousand dollars. He
> couldn't pay up, so the king ordered the man, along
> with his wife, children, and goods, to be auctioned
> off at the slave market.
>
> The poor wretch threw himself at the king's feet
> and begged, "Give me a chance and I'll pay it all
> back." Touched by his plea, the king let him off,
> erasing the debt. (Matthew 18:23-27)

But that undeserved gift of forgiveness for his overwhelming indebtedness apparently had little impact on how that forgiven man treated others. That suddenly ungrateful man forgot about the mercy and grace extended to him when he encountered a brother who owed him a debt.

> The servant was no sooner out of the room when
> he came upon one of his fellow servants who owed
> him ten dollars. He seized him by the throat and
> demanded, "Pay up. Now!"
>
> The poor wretch threw himself down and
> begged, "Give me a chance and I'll pay it all back."

But he wouldn't do it. He had him arrested and
put in jail until the debt was paid. When the other
servants saw this going on, they were outraged and
brought a detailed report to the king.

The king summoned the man and said, "You evil
servant! I forgave your entire debt when you begged
me for mercy. Shouldn't you be compelled to be mer-
ciful to your fellow servant who asked for mercy?"

The king was furious and put the screws to the
man until he paid back his entire debt. And that's
exactly what my Father in heaven is going to do to
each one of you who doesn't forgive unconditionally
anyone who asks for mercy. (Matthew 18:28-35)

I am generally fair and generous regarding money and forgiving
debts. But the problem with that little self-righteous pat on the back
is that I am missing the entire point of the parable.

It's not about money. It is about forgiveness. I am the debtor
with a sin debt that I could never begin to pay. I am the man who
begged for forgiveness of my debt over thirty years ago, and Jesus
granted that forgiveness. And I am the man who has sometimes
repaid His gracious gift by refusing to forgive those who have offended
or hurt me.

I have spent a lot of unhappy moments outside of fellowship
with my Lord because I did not want to forgive someone who hurt
me. I am grieved to think of how I have stubbornly refused to forgive
others for real and/or perceived slights over the years. I can imagine
Jesus looking at me with sadness because I have not fully compre-
hended the magnitude of the debt that has been erased from my

account because of Him. I picture His sadness not as judgment, but as sadness because I have missed out on the joy and peace He desires for me. There they were right in front of my spiritual nose, and I chose to hold on to bitterness.

Am I beating myself up? No. I think I am just being honest about the depth of my indebtedness to Christ. I hope I never lose sight of the gift of forgiveness.

FORGIVENESS FACTS

It doesn't take a theological genius to point out our need to forgive. I would imagine that many of you have struggled with the same unflinching commands in Scripture that I have. Part of my difficulty was a false impression of what forgiveness looks and feels like in real life. Let's examine what forgiveness is…and isn't.

Fact 1: Our Ability to Forgive Is Rooted in the Depth of Our Gratitude

The parable above is the basis for our first fact. The foundation of forgiveness is our gratitude for the undeserved forgiveness we have received through Christ. Take some time to meditate on how much you have been forgiven. In the gospel of Luke, we read about a sinful woman (perhaps a prostitute) who washed Jesus's feet with her tears and dried them with her hair. Jesus said:

> Impressive, isn't it? She was forgiven many, many sins, and so she is very, very grateful. If the forgiveness is minimal, the gratitude is minimal. (7:47)

Philip Yancey wrote about how Jesus always demonstrated forgiveness to the hurting: "I can't help noticing the tenderness with which Jesus treated people with wounds caused by moral failure. A Samaritan woman with five failed marriages, a dishonest tax collector, an adulteress, a prostitute, a disciple who denied Him—all these received from Jesus forgiveness and reinstatement, not the judgment they deserved. Jesus saw in people not what they had been but what they could be, not their past but their future."[5]

Christ has extended the same forgiveness toward us. It is an awesome act of grace that should fill us with a gratitude that overflows into a willingness to forgive others.

Fact 2: Forgiveness Is an Act of Trusting God for Justice

Forgiving is not the same as condoning or diminishing an offense. Forgiving people who have wronged you does not mean they are off the hook for any consequences or judgment that may result from their actions. Forgiveness is a personal act of *your* will that releases the other person from *your* condemnation. That is all Jesus asks of you; the offender is still responsible to God for the rest. By extending forgiveness, you are not saying the offense was insignificant or unimportant. You are saying that you trust God to see that justice is dispensed according to His holy judgment and timing rather than yours.

Fact 3: Forgiveness Does Not Require Amnesia

Forgiveness is not forgetting. The old "forgive and forget" admonition was one of the biggest barriers I faced in my journey toward learning how to forgive. You know the old mental challenge: Try not to picture an elephant in the room. You can't do it. Instantly the image pops into your mind. The more I tried to be spiritually mature by forgiving and forgetting, the more my offender became an elephant in the room. That person or event was all I could think of.

In time, if you entrust your need for justice to God, you will think less and less of the hurt or the offense. C. S. Lewis wrote to a friend late in his life: "Dear Mary… Do you know, only a few weeks ago, I realized suddenly that I had at last forgiven the cruel schoolmaster who so darkened my childhood. I had been trying to do it for years."[6] To try to achieve a state of forgetfulness is to set yourself up for failure and frustration.

I must add, however, that while it is impossible to instantly forget, we cannot use past hurts as hammers against others. A man was complaining about his wife to his buddy: "Whenever we get in a fight, she gets historical." His friend corrected him, "You mean hysterical." He said, "Nope, historical. She dredges up my past and reminds me of everything I've done wrong in our marriage." You may not forget the offense, but you can choose not to hold it against that person. Don't get historical.

Fact 4: Forgiveness Does Not Require Reunion

Forgiveness and reconciliation are not the same. Certainly it is a worthy goal to have the gift of forgiveness lead to the restoration of a damaged relationship. But it takes two people to reconcile, and you have no control over anyone's actions except your own. Your offenders may not respond graciously to your forgiveness. They may not be ready to acknowledge their part in the offense, accept forgiveness, or desire to be reconciled. Again, all that is required of you is to extend the grace of forgiveness.

Fact 5: Forgiveness Is an Act of Humility, Not Martyrdom

Remember, forgiveness is an overflow of gratitude for how much we have been forgiven. If I put on a mournful face and declare that I will forgive my brother "because someone has to be mature and take the bullet," well, that is not quite what Jesus had in mind.

Puffing myself up with the false humility of martyrdom (for example, [heavy sigh], "I guess I have to be the 'Christian' here") is not forgiveness. That attitude cannot restore me to my brother or to my Lord. Thomas Merton translated the sayings of spiritual sages from the fourth century whose wisdom is applicable to believers even today: "One of the elders was asked what was humility, and he said: If you forgive a brother who has injured you before he himself asks pardon."[7]

YOU'RE NO IDIOT, BUT...

Publishers have made a lot of money with book titles like *Skydiving for Dummies* (redundant) and *The Idiot's Guide to Idiots*. I humbly offer to you my own miniature edition called *The Goober's Guide to Forgiveness:*

- *Chapter 1: Exercise your will.* Forgiveness is an act of the will. It is not a response to feelings. Forgiveness requires choice and faith, just like every miracle. If we decide to wait until we "feel" like forgiving (or, worse, wait until the other person makes the first move), we will remain spiritually stuck. We must choose to forgive and then trust God to eventually change our feelings. The Holy Spirit will reshape our feelings over the course of time.

- *Chapter 2: Acknowledge the offense.* Jesus is not asking us to ignore reality. After all, if we have not been wronged, there is nothing to forgive. He is asking us to acknowledge how much we have been forgiven and to extend the same courtesy to others. Forgiveness is acknowledging the offense without cover-up or excuse and still choosing to forgive.
- *Chapter 3: Admit the hurt.* Forgiveness is not denial of the hurt. Pride will often cause us to not give the person who hurt us the "satisfaction" of knowing we are wounded. That is absurd. Acknowledge the reality of the injury, but make the choice to be healed.
- *Chapter 4: Give up revenge.* Forgiveness eliminates revenge as an option. The late author Lewis Smedes made a brilliant point about revenge. No matter how much we try, "We cannot get even; this is the inner fatality of revenge." When we start trying to get even, we have lost. How many times must I gossip about you to get even for the hurt you caused me? When is the scale even? Or do I need to have the scale tip a bit toward me to be satisfied? What a self-defeating pursuit that becomes! And the truth proclaimed by author Josh Billings is "there is no revenge so complete as forgiveness."
- *Chapter 5: Let go of the need to know.* Forgiving hurt without explanation is part of the faith-tour contract we signed when we decided to follow Jesus. Author David Stoop noted, "People choose the Path of Bitterness when they get caught up in trying to understand the reasons for the offense. They think, if only they could understand *why* the other person did

what he or she did, they could get over it and let it go."[8]

I have three words for that approach: *does not work.*

- *Chapter 6: Let go of the need to be right.* Forgiveness requires humility. We can be 100 percent right about an issue and lose every relationship around us in the process. Or we can be just as right but exercise grace and humility and not leave a trail of battered sheep in the dust.

- *Chapter 7: Begin to bless those who hurt us and pray good things for them.* This may be my least favorite requirement. But Jesus said: "When someone gives you a hard time, respond with the energies of prayer for that person" (Luke 6:28). I do not like to do this. The last thing I feel like doing is praying for the people who hurt me. But here's a secret: Praying for our enemies changes our attitude about them.

When I was a kid, I was a voracious reader of comic books (certainly one factor that explains my intellectual prowess). One of the advertisements that captivated me while reading those volumes was the little ad in the back of the comic book for the Incredible X-Ray Glasses. I imagined that with these amazing glasses, I could see through walls. I will confess that not all of my intentions for the glasses were pure, but I was sure that with the x-ray glasses I could see people in a way I never had seen them before. I would suggest this is how forgiveness works. We put on the glasses of gratitude and grace, and we see people who hurt us not as the enemy but as weak, fallible, needy people just like us. We look through their outer garments of pride and confusion and see the naked truth of their sin. They are people who need forgiveness (just like me), who perhaps have not reached the point in God's timing to be able to administer forgiveness (just like me a lot of the time). They are sinners saved by grace…just like me and you. A key component of forgiveness is to not make the other person evil. The people who did not allow our terminally ill daughter Katie to stay in the nursery were not bad people. They were fallible and fearful people just like me, and to demonize them would have made forgiveness impossible.

Paul wrote in the book of Romans that we should bless our enemies. The word "bless" can be translated to mean "to speak well of." Now, Paul understood life in the trenches. He knew that we can smile that tight-lipped smile and say polite things about those who hurt us and all the while be murmuring out the side of our mouth. So he threw the big punch right after the semicolon: "Bless your enemies; no cursing under your breath" (12:14).

Busted! Did I say that out loud? Anyway, blessing our adversaries messes with their minds, so at least we get that satisfaction. As Abe Lincoln sagely asked, "Am I not destroying my enemies when I make friends of them?"[9] The Christian paraphrase is: The best way to destroy your enemy is to bless him in prayer. One of my favorite quotes relating to this issue comes from Pastor R. G. Lee: "Men may spurn our appeals, reject our message, oppose our arguments, despise our persons; but they are helpless against our prayers."[10]

General Robert E. Lee was asked what he thought about a fellow officer. The man in question had been most unkind in his remarks about Lee, yet the general rated him as being "very satisfactory." The person confronting Lee was astounded. "General," he chided, "I guess you don't know what he's been saying about you." "I know," Lee responded, "but I was asked my opinion of him, not his opinion of me."[11] That, my friend, is the grace of God in action.

- *Chapter 8: Be selfish and forgive.* Say what? I have heard bitterness described as drinking rat poison and hoping the other person dies. Who wants that? I also appreciate the insight of author Hannah More who wrote, "Forgiveness is the economy of the heart.... Forgiveness saves the expense of anger, the cost of hatred, the waste of spirits."[12] When we follow the directive of Jesus and forgive, we are free to concentrate on the blessings in our lives.

YOU ARE FREE TO GO

Lewis Smedes often said that only forgiveness can "release us from the grip of our history." We cannot change an abusive upbringing. We cannot alter dysfunctional theological training that denied grace. We cannot simply ignore the hurts that have been visited upon us and be spiritually free. Only forgiveness can release us from the grip of these real and historical events.

A recent news story offered me a poignant illustration of being stuck in bitterness and anger. An Indian man spent more than eight years in prison because nobody told him he was free to go. Pratap Nayak, twenty-eight, was jailed for assault back in 1994 but was later declared innocent of the charge. Officials forgot to tell him the good news. "No one bothered about me, not even my own family," says Nayak. "They spoiled my life."[13]

I have to admit that at first I chuckled. Then I thought about the tragedy of that story. A man who could have been free lost eight years of his life. And he is obviously (and understandably) bitter. His quote was sobering: "No one bothered about me, not even my own family." It is interesting that Mr. Nayak seems equally upset about the imprisonment and his family's desertion. There is an interesting parallel between this poor man's experience and what we Christians do to ourselves.

We spend years and even lifetimes imprisoned by our lack of forgiveness. If we understand and apply the power that Jesus gave us, we are free to go forward in forgiveness and love. But instead we remain in the dingy, dark cell of bitterness. Sometimes it is because our family (the church) hasn't told us we are literally free to go forward in Christ. We have been declared innocent of the charges against us, and we need to trust Christ to empower us to declare others innocent as well. As Lewis Smedes noted, "Forgiveness is setting a prisoner free and then realizing the prisoner was you."[14]

I pray that all of us who have lost days, months, years, and decades imprisoned by our lack of forgiveness and our hate will give them up to the One who understands completely. The door is unlocked. But we must choose to open even an unlocked door. It won't swing open supernaturally. You have the power and ability to choose to open that jail door and step into the freedom of forgiveness. Is it worth it to harbor those feelings that affect your happiness, peace, and relationships with others? Will you regret on your deathbed (I know I will) those hours you were imprisoned by anger and hurt when your release had already been granted?

A friend told me her story of woundedness. If her story was accurate (and I suspect it was), she had every right to expect the other party to ask her forgiveness and reconciliation, though she admitted to contributing to the split. A long period of anger, hurt, and awkward evasion had transpired. I suggested to her that she was responsible only for her own actions. Had she done anything to exacerbate the situation that might prompt *her* to seek forgiveness from the other party? My friend went and asked forgiveness for her wrongdoing without mentioning any of the seemingly obvious transgressions against her and without a martyr's attitude. She was thrilled to report that her act of grace resulted in a reconciliation. The other party was so relieved to see her address the issue without rancor that he also sought her forgiveness.

Such results are not guaranteed. Some people will refuse your attempt. Some will accept your desire for forgiveness with a condescending "it's about time" attitude. At that point you must walk away and know that you have been obedient to Christ's commands. Focus on Him. You sought not what you wanted but what He wanted. Thinking that way makes a difference in your attitude.

I read about a Sunday-school teacher who finished her lesson on forgiveness and decided to review. "Can anyone tell me what you must do before you can be forgiven of sin?" There was an uncomfortable silence before a little voice volunteered, "We have to sin."

I think we have pretty much all fulfilled that. I know I'm in. As I become more aware of what Jesus has done for me, I respond to Him more like the tax collector who realized the magnitude of his sin.

> Meanwhile the tax man, slumped in the shadows, his
> face in his hands, not daring to look up, said, "God,
> give mercy. Forgive me, a sinner." (Luke 18:13)

That kind of humble spirit allows us to forgive. The apostle Paul's word to the church at Galatia is a great place to end this chapter.

If someone falls into sin, forgivingly restore him, saving your critical comments for yourself. You might be needing forgiveness before the day's out. (Galatians 6:1)

Sixteenth-century English author Thomas Fuller observed, "He that cannot forgive others breaks the bridge over which he must pass himself; for every man has to be forgiven."[15] A Christian who is not forgiving is a Christian who is not growing. Make the choice to forgive. God will do the rest.

— For Reflection and Discussion —

1. Why is forgiveness sometimes so incredibly difficult?
2. Why did Jesus tie forgiveness of our own sins to our willingness to forgive others?
3. In what ways can a lack of forgiveness stunt spiritual growth?
4. Review the list of what forgiveness is and isn't. What misconceptions have you had about forgiveness? In what ways has correcting them affected your ability to forgive?
5. Read Romans 12:14. Why does Paul tell us to pray for those who make our lives difficult?
6. Ask Jesus to examine your heart and reveal if you need to forgive someone. Ask Him now to help you forgive that person by faith and to begin to change your heart toward him or her. Bless that person in prayer each day.

—Part III—

REUNITED AND
IT FEELS SO GOOD

Sticking Together—Forever

Chapter 10

REPEAT AFTER ME: "I HAVE THE RIGHT TO NOTHING"

Taking Responsibility for Ourselves and One Another

We've gotten to the point where everybody's got a right and nobody's got a responsibility.

NEWTON MINOW, FORMER CHAIRMAN
OF THE FEDERAL COMMUNICATIONS COMMISSION

J ayde Hanson of London, England, accidentally wounded his girl-friend in front of over one million viewers during a televised circus performance. Hanson was attempting to throw as many knives as possible at Yana Rodianova in sixty seconds without hitting her. But one errant throw grazed her head. Stagehands rushed to assist the bleeding woman. Her wound was only superficial, but Rodianova decided to forgo any future involvement with Hanson's vocation.

Perhaps her decision was assisted by his less-than-apologetic response. Hanson defiantly noted, "In eleven years of performing, I've only hit my assistant on five occasions."[1]

Aren't we like that a lot of the time? "Hey, I've been a Christian for eleven years, and I only wounded someone on five occasions." Not good enough. We need to take responsibility and repair the damage promptly. There are no excuses for a person who wants to be a representative of Jesus Christ. Allow John to speak for me:

> On the other hand, if we admit our sins—make a
> clean breast of them—[Christ] won't let us down;
> he'll be true to himself. He'll forgive our sins and
> purge us of all wrongdoing. (1 John 1:9)

One of my consistent drumbeats is that Christians need to quit making excuses for the wounds they've inflicted and start owning up to the responsibilities assumed when they took the sacred title Christian. A couple of years ago, I was directing a Texas Rangers game and I was a...how do you say "jerk" nicely? I made some remarks about a camera operator that were unprofessional and unkind. (Hey, as an American I have the right to say what I think. Right?) Well, he found out what I said. That night at the hotel I considered my response. I decided to seek him out the next day, apologize, and ask forgiveness for my Bad Christian day.

I don't feel God often speaks to me in an audible voice. But this was one of those times when I clearly heard His prompting: "You embarrassed him publicly, and you must apologize publicly." I did not want to do that. But the next day I went to the crew break room, prayed, swallowed my pride (I gained about fifty pounds), and went in to apologize. In front of the production crew, I asked him to forgive me for my comments. He was gracious and told me I didn't have to do that. But I did. I had done damage, and I had a responsibility to repent and do my best to repair it.

RIGHTS OR RESPONSIBILITIES?

One of biggest obstacles keeping American Christians from taking responsibility for their actions is this sacred American ideal that we all have rights. I found nearly six thousand Web sites with the phrase "rights of American citizens" contained in the text. Our sacred Bill of Rights proclaims we have the right of free speech. We have the right to bear arms and the right to free assembly. We in the United States believe that we have the right to the pursuit of happiness. We are read our rights when arrested—or so I hear. We have a right to representation and the right to freedom of religion. All of these constitutional rights for citizens are wonderful, and we are blessed to have them.

Look up the definition of *rights,* and you will find that it is something due us by tradition, governmental law, or moral principle. But I fear that we Christians have begun to confuse our legitimate rights as citizens with our responsibilities as followers of Christ. The "rights" mentality sneaks into our church mind-set in insidious ways. The truth is that we forfeit our American idea of rights when we decide to follow Christ, and we add the uncomfortable truth of responsibility to our journey. (I am not talking about our legal rights as Christians in schools, in the workplace, and so on. That is a different issue covered much better by writers like Charles Colson.)

What actually is "due" us when we sign on in faith to follow Jesus? I think that faulty teaching, a lack of knowledge of God's Word, and the slick presentation of the "prosperity" gospel have led us to assume that we do have rights as a part of the deal. We are told, for example, we have the right to financial security if we give money to the Lord (usually with the caveat that certain ministries are the approved vendors of those blessings). But Scripture tells us we have the responsibility to give, and when we do, our needs will be met. That is a very different concept. Items on our wish list are not dispensed on demand. Some teachers today say we have the right to good health if we are faithful. But Scripture suggests only that we *might* receive healing from our physical ailments. In reality, God's answer to a prayer for healing might be strength and grace to endure the illness.

This past weekend I was privileged to watch a remarkable man demonstrate how God gives us strength and grace in the midst of overwhelming trouble. The Texas Rangers major league baseball team introduced its first franchise Hall of Fame class, which included fine players such as Nolan Ryan, pitcher Charlie Hough, and my friend, catcher Jim Sundberg. But the most memorable moment came when former manager Johnnie Oates was introduced to a luncheon crowd. His body was ravaged by a cancerous brain tumor that was incurable. But his spirit was as bright as the Texas sunshine filtering into the hotel. Oates shared his faith with a dignity that moved the most cynical in the room. His supernatural courage and peace spoke volumes to everyone that there was something different about this man. And Johnnie Oates made it clear that the "something" was his abiding faith in Jesus Christ.

I have no way of knowing for sure in this life, but I wonder if God doesn't allow uncommon men like Johnnie to go through such afflictions so that we can see firsthand what real faith looks like in the flesh. Jesus made a difference in Johnnie Oates's life, and that allowed Johnnie to make a difference in the lives of people who witnessed his strength and dignity. At times I wonder if I would pass the test with such grace. If the time comes, I know the Good Shepherd will be there at my side.

When we drag the American consumer mind-set into the church of Jesus Christ, we create problems. Yes, we attend our local church in part to have our needs met. But I know people who shop for churches the way I look for a good restaurant. If they get bad service at church, they won't be coming back. If customer service (the elder board) doesn't grant them satisfaction, then "fine," they'll find a church that will listen. And, by the way, if the church doesn't want their advice, then apparently it doesn't want their business (tithe) either.

The always candid James lays it out in plain language:

> Where do you think all these appalling wars and quar-
> rels come from? Do you think they just happen? Think
> again. They come about because you want your own
> way, and fight for it deep inside yourselves. (4:1)

American culture has put such a high value on entitlement and compensation for both real and perceived wrongs that this way of thinking permeates our society. We have all heard of absurd amounts of money given to victims who were injured because of their own careless neglect. Humor columnist Dave Barry wrote about this trend. "Fortunately, I live in the United States of America, where we are gradually coming to understand that nothing we do is ever our fault, especially if it is really stupid."[2] The confusion between rights and responsibilities creates a dangerous trap for the body of Christ. Let me help sort it out: Rights are what are due to us as followers of Christ. (Basically, we have none.) Responsibilities are what are due to our fellow believers because we are one in Christ. (Basically, being responsible is an act of love and obedience.) What will happen if we confuse rights with responsibilities? Then all our search-and-rescue efforts will be for nothing in the long run because we won't have learned how to lay down our lives for one another.

Let's look at our responsibilities to one another as followers of Jesus.

We Have a Responsibility to Love Our Fellow Members of the Flock

The apostle John offered some insight on this subject:

> If anyone boasts, "I love God," and goes right on hating his brother or sister, thinking nothing of it, he is a liar. If he won't love the person he can see, how can he love the God he can't see? The command we have from Christ is blunt: Loving God includes loving people. You've got to love both. (1 John 4:20-21)

The command is indeed blunt. Noted Christian preacher A. B. Simpson once stated that "a good way to test your love to God is by the way you treat your brother.... God is more concerned by my conduct toward my brother than by my prayers to Him."[3]

Jesus said something similar to the Pharisees:

> Do you want to stand out? Then step down. Be a servant. If you puff yourself up, you'll get the wind

knocked out of you. But if you're content to simply
be yourself, your life will count for plenty. (Matthew
23:11-12)

I have witnessed some embarrassingly bad treatment of service personnel by Christian leaders and very pious religious people. As for me, I believe my walk with Jesus is easily measured by how I treat waiters, clerks, and others in the service industry. (Remember, that person who is providing slow or sloppy service is a person whom Jesus died on the cross to save.) Considering the incredible grace and forgiveness that God has demonstrated toward us, any follower of Christ exhibits astounding arrogance when he or she treats others gracelessly. I have no idea of the life circumstances of the people who serve me in the course of any day. Perhaps they are carrying overwhelming, nearly incapacitating burdens. Maybe they are ill-equipped for the job, but they have no other option for providing for their basic needs or the needs of their family. Often, when a gentle reminder or kind request is all that is needed to defuse the moment, we drop a sarcastic or mean comment instead, and then further communicate our disgust by leaving a small gratuity. We have a responsibility as representatives of Jesus to be kind to everyone we encounter in our daily journeys. We can certainly be bold in our requests for service, but we are not at liberty to be obnoxious.

All that people you treated unkindly will remember was that religious person who flamboyantly bowed to say grace or complained loudly about being made late for Bible study. They will chalk this experience up in the category of hypocrisy they encounter in their daily travails. And the startling paradox of asking grace but granting none will not be lost on them.

We Have a Responsibility to Demonstrate Humility

In his letter to Timothy, the apostle Paul humbly noted:

> Here is a trustworthy saying that deserves full accep-
> tance: Christ Jesus came into the world to save sin-
> ners—of whom I am the worst. (1 Timothy 1:15, NIV)

That kind of humility shows Paul's lack of pride and is not at all self-deprecating. In my experience, true humility is a reliable indicator of a person who is walking with Christ. Author William P. Farley wrote, "Humility always metamorphoses into something more beautiful; it is the fountainhead of the other virtues."[4] I think that is correct. People who display the holiness that I desire in my own life are always, I repeat *always,* set apart by their humility.

Humility paired with love allows us to follow the advice Paul sent to the church at Galatia:

> Stoop down and reach out to those who are op-
> pressed. Share their burdens, and so complete
> Christ's law. (Galatians 6:2)

The interesting phrase there is "stoop down." You have to put aside a bit of pride in order to stoop down to help. Author John E. Southard made the interesting observation that the only "people with whom you should try to get even are those who have helped you."[5]

We Have a Responsibility to Speak Well of Our Brothers and Sisters

Imagine the worst period of your Christian walk—and then imagine how you would feel if that time frame became the basis for how you were judged and evaluated by your Christian brothers and sisters. Well, some of the lambs around you may be exactly at that point in their own lives. They need to have their wounds bound and treated, not picked at and reopened. Paul, in his famous love chapter, wrote that love "doesn't keep score of the sins of others" (1 Corinthians 13:5). It is time for us to remove the big tally board from our mental playing field.

When we keep track of others' sins, we are prone to speak ill of them and gossip about them when grace and patience is in order. When I put someone else down, that's a clear indication I need to check myself into the Bible Repair Shop to have my pride levels checked (usually I'm a couple of quarts over). I agree with Joel Belz, CEO of *World* magazine, who wrote, "The inclination to put someone else down is almost always rooted in our determination to lift ourselves up and to perch ourselves on some lofty and prominent peak."[6]

I think the apostle James developed the original No Spin Zone (apologies to Bill O'Reilly). His words are always to the point and valuable. On this issue James wrote:

> You can develop a healthy, robust community that lives
> right with God and enjoy its results *only* if you do the
> hard work of getting along with each other, treating
> each other with dignity and honor. (James 3:18)

In *Fresh Wind, Fresh Fire,* pastor Jim Cymbala observed, "I know what most easily destroys churches. It's not crack cocaine, government oppression or even lack of funds. Rather it's gossip and slander that grieves the Holy Spirit." All I can add is "ouch" and "amen" in that order. We can get quite an aerobic workout jumping to conclusions and running people down. Paul advised his flock in Corinth to slow down and get the facts before they shot off their mouths:

> All I'm doing right now, friends, is showing how these things pertain to Apollos and me so that you will learn restraint and not rush into making judgments without knowing all the facts. It's important to look at things from God's point of view. I would rather not see you inflating or deflating reputations based on mere hearsay. (1 Corinthians 4:6)

May I expose another mutation of the gossip virus? That would be prayer and "sharing" as gossip. When we tell each other about a brother or sister in Christ who is struggling, we don't need to go into the tabloid version of the story. All we need to say is something like, "Please pray for Joe. He is going through a hard time and needs your prayer." Cool. What I don't need is, "Please pray for Joe. He is having an affair with Jane, and Jim Johnson saw him coming out of a gentleman's bar last night." Sharing a detailed "prayer request" with those who don't really know Joe borders precariously on gossip. I am pretty confident that God is already aware of Joe's story. When we pray, we don't have to remind Him of the details. Be careful and be loving when sharing prayer requests. When Joe realizes that everyone knows every detail of his struggle, he will be even less likely to return to the place that should offer him healing and redemption.

We Have a Responsibility to Cheer About the Success of Others

Author Harold Coffin wrote, "Envy is the art of counting the other fellow's blessings instead of your own."[7] To be envious of another's success prevents us from receiving what God has for us—so we perceive that He can't meet our needs and that His promises are empty. And again we come back to the subject of God's sovereignty and the question of whether we actually believe He is. For many years I was envious of some who had moved into television jobs that I felt I was qualified to perform. Now I can see that had I moved into those positions, I likely would not have had the opportunity to write. My initial envy was actually a lack of trust in God's best for me, mixed in, of course, with the ever-present pride.

> Make a careful exploration of who you are and the
> work you have been given, and then sink yourself
> into that. Don't be impressed with yourself. Don't
> compare yourself with others. (Galatians 6:4)

I pray that we will not compare ourselves to others. God made me a unique creation with a combination of talents and spiritual gifts selected especially for me. He did the same for you. What an exciting voyage to discover all that God has destined and gifted us to do. Plus, the realization that God has a personal destiny for me changes my perspective and allows me to rejoice in the success of others.

We Have a Responsibility to Be Tenacious in Our Faith

I believe that sometimes hanging in there is all God requires of us. I like to use the image of fictional boxer Rocky Balboa from the first *Rocky* movie as a good example of what it means to give faith more credence than feelings. Rocky is getting pummeled in the ring, but he keeps getting up. You expect him to give up, but he gets up every time. That is how a Christian's faith sometimes plays itself out. Like

Rocky, we pick ourselves up off the mat in faith that the Lord will honor our effort. I am pretty sure that Rocky did not feel like getting up time after time. He simply made the decision to continue. For him, this was a predetermined choice. A given.

One of the things that I have taught all my sons is that they have to make most of their important decisions in advance. You have to choose in advance not to get in a car with a group of young men who have been drinking, or peer pressure just might cause you to stumble. You have to choose in advance to put a filter on your Internet software before temptation overpowers will. I chose in advance not to join a group of television colleagues who liked to visit gentlemen's clubs. When we base our lives and decisions on a solid knowledge of God's Word, having integrated it into our moral fabric, about 95 percent of our decisions are made before we ever face an actual choice.

Many times I have not felt like getting up off the mat. It would have been far easier to stay down and give up. But Christ calls us on to victory. If we make the decision ahead of time to get back up when we're knocked down, getting up will be easier. This tenacious clinging to Jesus is an example that lets wounded lambs see how faith plays out in real life. And we should pray to be just as tenacious in our desire to not give up on the wounded and abandoned lambs from our flock.

We Have a Responsibility to Go After the Wandering Lambs

I hope by now you have come to believe the importance of this particular task. Let's see what my man James has for us:

> My dear friends, if you know people who have wandered off from God's truth, don't write them off. Go

after them. Get them back and you will have rescued precious lives from destruction and prevented an epidemic of wandering away from God. (James 5:19-20)

Here is my challenge to all of us. Don't write off the wandering and wounded lambs. Many wonderful people have wandered away from God's truth. Let's go after them. If the number of sheep leaving the flock is not already epidemic, it is getting uncomfortably close.

We Have a Responsibility to Give Up Our Rights for the Unity of the Flock

We must take responsibility for our actions. There is an amazing sense of relief when we take responsibility, repent, repair the damage where needed, and rejoice in the process. No longer do we have to invest energy in covering our respective seating areas. All I have to do is make the choice to forfeit my rights and accept my responsibility as a representative of Jesus.

The apostle Paul was a tough guy. I would consider him a man's man, honest, confrontational, and direct. Paul's letter to the church in Corinth could be written today to the church in Chicago or Chillicothe or Garland or (insert your town here). Had Paul written the letter to me at a time when I felt my rights were being violated, I would have had a pretty strong reaction to it. For your entertainment, I have added in italics what those reactions might have been:

> Now, regarding the one who started all this—the person in question who caused all this pain—I want you to know that I am not the one injured in this as much as, with a few exceptions, all of you. *[Darn*

right! This jerk caused a lot of pain for me while you were on the road, Paul. He is clearly guilty, and I am the one who has had to live with him.] So I don't want to come down too hard. What the majority of you agreed to as punishment is punishment enough. *[Well, I'm not sure he has really learned his lesson. I know I will never trust him again.]* Now is the time to forgive this man and help him back on his feet. If all you do is pour on the guilt, you could very well drown him in it. *[Easy for you to say! You're in Rome. You haven't been here, and I don't think you really understand how much he hurt me. (Soft violin music plays in background.)]* My counsel now is to pour on the love. *[What?! Are you nuts? Love him? After what he did to me? Do you remember what he did to me? You expect me to love him? It will take a miracle for me just to tolerate him!]*

The focus of my letter wasn't on punishing the offender but on getting you to take responsibility for the health of the church. *[Oh, I see. You're going to lay it all on me. It's my responsibility. What about that blankety-blank's responsibility? He's got responsibility too, right? What about that, Mr. Super Spiritual?]* So if you forgive him, I forgive him. Don't think I'm carrying around a list of personal grudges. *[Well yeah, you don't know him. Why is this on my shoulders? Does anyone around here remember that I am the one who got hurt? Hello?]* The fact is that I'm joining in with *your* forgiveness, as Christ is with us, guiding us. *[Oh, here it*

is: the guilt trip. What took you so long?] After all, we
don't want to unwittingly give Satan an opening for
yet more mischief—we're not oblivious to his sly ways!
*[I'm giving Satan an opening? Did you actually say that?
How about that little minion of Satan that nearly destroyed me? What about him?]* (2 Corinthians 2:5-11)

Forgive me if that seemed a little over the top. But I think the
honesty of it is important. That kind of response is the one that often
comes out of the dark corners of my heart where Jesus is working hard
to try to illuminate what's really in my nature: a tendency not to take
responsibility for my actions. Every one of us is responsible for his or
her own actions. We all will be judged accordingly. I can control only
one aspect of my universe: my responses.

Let's review my response to Paul's letter now that I am a mature
and sanctified Christian author. (Oops, my Pharisee Meter just
peaked.) Seriously, this is how I need to take responsibility and
respond when I realize with gratitude how much I have been forgiven:

Now, regarding the one who started all this—the person in question who caused all this pain—I want you
to know that I am not the one injured in this as
much as, with a few exceptions, all of you. *[Thank
you for your gracious acknowledgment of my hurt. It
means a lot that you care and have taken the time to
express that.]* So I don't want to come down too hard.
What the majority of you agreed to as punishment is
punishment enough. Now is the time to forgive this
man and help him back on his feet. *[I agree. It is time*

to forgive, move on, and demonstrate the love of Christ that we trying to proclaim.] If all you do is pour on the guilt, you could very well drown him in it. *[It is not my heart's desire to destroy another brother or sister in Christ to gain revenge for my hurt. My strength and comfort are in Christ.]* My counsel now is to pour on the love. *[Pray for me to have the power of Christ in me to do that. I know that is what will honor my Lord, and it is my desire to serve Him by supernaturally showing His amazing grace to a person I can't love in my own power. I must be honest: I don't feel like forgiving this person, but I will claim that forgiveness in faith and by the strength of Christ living through me.]*

The focus of my letter wasn't on punishing the offender but on getting you to take responsibility for the health of the church. *[Amen. It is my responsibility to care and to do all I can to make this place a hospital for those in need.]* So if you forgive him, I forgive him. Don't think I'm carrying around a list of personal grudges. The fact is that I'm joining in with your forgiveness, as Christ is with us, guiding us. *[I do forgive him. I have so much to be grateful for because I—who am without merit—have been forgiven so much.]* After all, we don't want to unwittingly give Satan an opening for yet more mischief—we're not oblivious to his sly ways! *[God forbid that my lack of forgiveness and lack of gratitude do any damage to His wonderful name and the message of His salvation and grace. Lord, give me the strength to accept the hurt and forgive because of my love for You!]*

A little bit of a difference in the tone of those responses, huh? If we take time to be still and meditate on how much we have been forgiven, I would suspect the second response would be possible.

Remember the example of the women's basketball team way back in the introduction? That team was looking forward to restoring its wounded players so that they could join the brand-new recruits and returning veterans on the court. Combined, they would be a great team. My desire for us is that we restore the wounded even as we recruit new converts to Christ. How much more could we accomplish for our Lord if we embraced our responsibilities and marshaled all of our assets? Call me crazy, but I believe we can do a lot more.

— For Reflection and Discussion —

1. What are some cultural rights that we tend to confuse as "Christian" rights?
2. Why is humility such a benchmark of maturity in Christ?
3. What are the dangers of gossip in the body of Christ? How does Satan use gossip to divide the body?
4. What responsibilities to the flock are most difficult for you to fulfill? Select one to work on and write down two ways in which you will aim for improvement in that area. Ask a brother or sister you trust to encourage your efforts with prayer—and offer to do the same for them.
5. Reread 2 Corinthians 2:5-11. What lessons can you learn from Paul's letter to the church at Corinth about dealing with hurts—both your own and others'?

Chapter 11

THE ULTIMATE GIFT
OF GRATITUDE

Committing to the Cause

If we don't turn around now, we just may get where we're going.

NATIVE AMERICAN SAYING

The German philosopher (and pessimist) Arthur Schopenhauer once compared human beings to porcupines trying to gain warmth from each other on a frigid night. "The colder it gets outside, the more we huddle together for warmth; but the closer we get to one another, the more we hurt each other with our sharp quills. And in the lonely night of earth's winter eventually we begin to drift apart, wander out on our own and freeze to death in our loneliness."[1] Isn't that a picture of how the body of Christ can function at times? Yeah, we will sometimes poke each other with our quills of selfishness, anger, or pride. But with the healing power of Jesus, the church can learn how to forgive, stay close, and keep warm in the fellowship of Christ.

We need each other in the body of Christ. As we move—and stay—closer together, keeping each other warm with the soft wool of our coats, we need to learn to zealously defend biblical truth, not our personal preferences. Paul fought the battle in Romans:

> Welcome with open arms fellow believers who don't see things the way you do. And don't jump all over them every time they do or say something you don't agree with—even when it seems that they are strong on opinions but weak in the faith department. Remember, they have their own history to deal with. Treat them gently.
>
> For instance, a person who has been around for a while might well be convinced that he can eat anything on the table, while another, with a different background, might assume all Christians should be vegetarians and eat accordingly. But since both are guests at Christ's table, wouldn't it be terribly rude if they fell to criticizing what the other ate or didn't eat? God, after all, invited them both to the table. Do you have any business crossing people off the guest list or interfering with God's welcome? If there are corrections to be made or manners to be learned, God can handle that without your help. (14:1-4)

Humility is the trait that will help us get this job done. "The church is not made up of spiritual giants," wrote author David J. Bosch in *A Spirituality of the Road*. "Only broken men can lead others to the cross."[2] We are all broken and damaged goods. That is the message of the Cross. And here's the power of it: Not only can people like you and me be redeemed, but we are valuable to God.

One of the interesting traits of this post-9/11 era is the mind-set that we should not change our lifestyles because of fear. If we allow evil to alter our lives, we have effectively "let the terrorists win." I think that mind-set should be integrated into the church.

When we allow any shepherd who hurts us to diminish our relationship with God, then we allow the ultimate terrorist, Satan, to win. If we stop attending church because of the unseemly actions of some churchgoers, the ultimate terrorist wins. If we hang on to bitterness and refuse to forgive, the ultimate terrorist wins. If we fail to pursue alienated lambs, the ultimate terrorist wins. If we are divided, the ultimate terrorist wins.

I hope this book has challenged you not to let any of these things happen. When you see others in the flock wandering away, I pray that you will pursue them with love and concern. When you are wounded, I pray that you will find the strength to forgive. And when you see other people hurting, I pray you will help them heal.

Our responsibility to each other is abidingly clear. We cannot put off until tomorrow what God requires of us today. We need to be there for each other with a caring presence and the affirmation of God's promises:

> If your heart is broken, you'll find GOD right there;
> if you're kicked in the gut, he'll help you catch your
> breath. (Psalm 34:18)

Everyone needs grace, love, and a body of believers who understands how to care, heal, and restore. And I believe that our profound gratitude to the Lord Jesus for the grace, love, and restoration He has made available to us compels us to share those gifts with others.

Have you ever been overwhelmed with gratitude for a gift or act of kindness? Scholar William Arthur Ward noted, "Feeling gratitude and not expressing it is like wrapping a gift and not giving it."[3] One of the gifts of gratitude we can give back to God is caring about and for His flock.

I am sure you have read all the works of Epictetus (who hasn't?) and are familiar with his quote, "God has entrusted me with myself." Put differently, God has given me to me, and I can use myself for His work, His lost lambs, His flock. I can make a small difference if I reach out to His lost and wandering lambs. That is what Jesus expects of me. The smallest action is far better than the biggest intention. The writer of Proverbs tells us:

> Never walk away from someone who deserves help;
>> your hand is *God's* hand for that person.
> Don't tell your neighbor, "Maybe some other time,"
>> or, "Try me tomorrow." (3:27-28)

Certainly the task can seem overwhelming, but we must remember that we are responsible only for ourselves. Helen Keller said it beautifully when she wrote, "I am only one; but still I am one. I cannot do everything, but still I can do something; I will not refuse to do the something I can do."[4] The apostle Paul noted that "each of you must take responsibility for doing the creative best you can with your own life" (Galatians 6:5). That is all we can do.

To the Corinthians, Paul wrote:

We're Christ's representatives. God uses us to persuade men and women to drop their differences and
enter into God's work of making things right between
them. We're speaking for Christ himself now: Become
friends with God; he's already a friend with you.
(2 Corinthians 5:20)

What an incredible concept and what a great place to end our
journey: "Become friends with God; he's already a friend with you."

I hope you will join me in the ministry to wounded lambs. If you
are a wounded lamb, I pray that you will come back to the flock. We
need you. We miss you. You matter.

NOTES

Chapter 1: Wounded and Abandoned

1. George Barna, from a press release for *Grow Your Church from the Outside In*, in *Barna Update*, www.barna.org, October 9, 2000.

2. George Barna, "Unchurched People," www. barna.org, 2000.

3. Rick Warren, quoted in Frank Lewis, "Preaching that Restores," *Leadership Journal*, Winter 2001, 43.

4. Keith Green, www.oneliners-and-proverbs.com, 2003.

Chapter 2: Lethargic Lambs

1. Jonathan Rauch, "Let It Be," *Atlantic Monthly* 291, no. 4, May 2003, 34.

2. Lena Wolter, quoted in Martin E. Marty, "Context," www.preachingtoday.com, August 10, 2003.

3. Elie Wiesel, *U.S. News & World Report*, October 27, 1986.

4. George Barna, "The Year's Most Intriguing Findings, from Barna Research Studies," www.barna.org, December 2001.

Chapter 3: Feud for Thought

1. Phillip Keller, *A Shepherd Looks at Psalm 23* (Grand Rapids: Zondervan, 1997), 37-40.

2. Frederick Buechner, *Whistling in the Dark* (New York: Harper-Collins, 1993), 37-38.

3. *Fox News* transcript, "The Beltway Boys," August 9, 2003.

4. Mary Hirsch, www.quotationspage.com, February 12, 2003.

Chapter 4: The Heart of a Shepherd

1. David Hansen, "Belgrade Community Church, Belgrade, Montana," *Leadership Journal,* Summer 1998, 36-38.

Chapter 5: Never Leave a Lamb Behind!

1. Michael J. Cusick, "A Conversation with Mike Yaconelli," *Mars Hill Review,* May 1995, 67-87.
2. George Barna, "Barna Identifies Seven Paradoxes Regarding America's Faith," www.barna.org, December 17, 2002.
3. John S. Savage, "Ministry to Missing Members," *Leadership Journal,* Fall 1996, 104.
4. Lyle Pointer, quoted in Howard Culbertson, "Exit Interview Guidelines and Suggestions," www.home.snu.edu/~hculbert.fs, July 20, 2003.
5. Mathew Woodley, "Chronically Wounded and Needy," *Leadership Journal,* Spring 1997, 53.
6. Dwight L. Carlson, "Exposing the Myth that Christians Should Not Have Emotional Problems," *Christianity Today,* February 9, 1998, 28.
7. Charles Spurgeon, "The Christian's Heaviness and Rejoicing," Sermon 222, www.spurgeon.org, October 19, 2003.
8. Charles Spurgeon, "The Cost of Being a Soul-Winner," www.spurgeon.org, October 19, 2003.

Chapter 6: Lambentations

1. Philip Yancey, "Guilt Good and Bad," *Christianity Today,* November 18, 2002, 112.
2. Dave McKenna, "Be a Pepper," www.washingtoncity paper.com, October 26, 2001.

Chapter 7: Your Bleating Heart (Will Tell On You)

1. Eugene O'Neill, quoted in Cyndi Haynes, *2002 Ways to Cheer Yourself Up* (Kansas City, MO: Andrews McMeel, 1998), 65.

2. Bill Bright, "Tips on How to Be Miserable," www.crosswalk .com, January 9, 2003.

3. Adam R. Holz, "Discipling the Broken," *Discipleship Journal*, September–October 2001, 62.

4. Corrie ten Boom, quoted in Amy E. Dean, *Peace of Mind: Daily Meditations for Easing Stress* (New York: Bantam, 1995), 51.

5. Stacey Padrick, "I Know God Is Good, But…," *Discipleship Journal*, May–June 2003, 23.

6. Alfred D'Souza, www.quoteserver.ca, April 26, 2003.

7. Charles Bracelen Flood, *Lee: The Last Years* (Boston: Houghton Mifflin, 1998), 136.

Chapter 8: You Haven't Got Time for the Pain

1. Frederick Buechner, *Wishful Thinking, A Seeker's ABC* (San Francisco: HarperCollins, 1993), 2.

2. C. S. Lewis, *Mere Christianity* (New York: Macmillan, 1952), 52-53.

Chapter 9: Forgiveness Is Not Optional

1. John Wesley, quoted in Greg Laurie, "Doing Our Duty," *Harvest Online*, www.greglaurie.org, August 1, 2001.

2. Mark Twain, www.theotherpages.org, April 30, 2002.

3. Steve Brown, "Only Sinners Welcome," www.crosswalk.com, 2002.

4. Marilyn Elias, "Psychologists Now Know What Makes People Happy," *USA Today,* December 9, 2002.

5. Philip Yancey, "God of the Maggies," *Christianity Today,* April 28, 2003, 88.

6. C. S. Lewis, *Letters to an American Lady* (Grand Rapids: Eerdmans, 1967), 117.

7. Thomas Merton, quoted in "Reflections," *Christianity Today,* June 2003, 49.

8. David Stoop, *Forgiving the Unforgivable* (Ann Arbor: Vine, 2003), 75.

9. Abraham Lincoln, www.wisdomquotes.com, 2003.

10. R. G. Lee, *Sermonic Library* (Orlando: Christ for the World, 1969), 101.

11. James S. Hewett, *Illustrations Unlimited* (Wheaton: Tyndale, 1988), 310.

12. Hannah More, "Christianity: A Practical Principle," *Practical Piety* (Baltimore: J. Kingston, 1812), quoted in "Reflections," *Christianity Today,* September 9, 2002, 68.

13. "It Must Be True," *The Week Magazine,* March 7, 2003, 12.

14. Lewis B. Smedes, *The Art of Forgiving* (New York: Ballantine, 1997), 178.

15. Thomas Fuller, www.brainyquote.com, 2003.

Chapter 10: Repeat After Me: "I Have the Right to Nothing"

1. "Quicktakes," *World,* April 19, 2003, 16.

2. Dave Barry, "The Dairy Worst Addiction There Is," *Dallas Morning News,* July 27, 2003.

3. A. B. Simpson, quoted in Norris Magnuson, *Salvation in the Slums* (Grand Rapids: Baker, 1990).

4. William P. Farley, "The Indispensable Virtue," *Discipleship Journal* 125, September–October 2001, 22.

5. John E. Southard, www.brainyquote.com, 2003.

6. Joel Belz, "The Pride Game," *World,* June 28, 2003, 5.

7. Harold Coffin, www.queenofquotes.com, June 24, 2002.

Chapter 11: The Ultimate Gift of Gratitude

1. Arthur Schopenhauer, quoted in Wayne Brouwer, "Forgiving Others," www.preachingtoday.com, 2003.

2. David J. Bosch, *A Spirituality of the Road* (Eugene, OR: Wipf and Stock, 2001), quoted in "Reflections," *Christianity Today,* June 2003, 49.

3. William Arthur Ward, www.quotegarden.com, 2003.

4. Helen Keller, www.brainyquote.com, 2003.

If you would like
to contact Dave Burchett,
please visit his Web site at
www.daveburchett.com.

God's Wisdom for the
WOUNDED

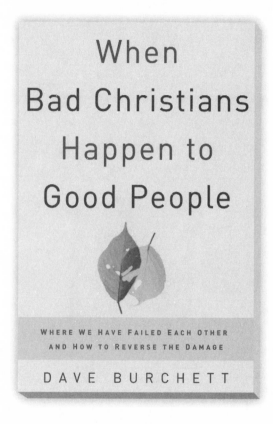

When
Bad Christians
Happen to
Good People

WHERE WE HAVE FAILED EACH OTHER
AND HOW TO REVERSE THE DAMAGE

DAVE BURCHETT

For years, people have rejected the church because of damaging encounters with Christians. *When Bad Christians Happen to Good People* is for every person who has ever been hurt and those responsible for inflicting damaging wounds.

Available in bookstores everywhere.

WATERBROOK PRESS
www.waterbrookpress.com